THE YOGA-SŪTRA OF PATAÑJALI

Selected Books by the Author

The Essence of Yoga

Lucid Waking

Structures of Consciousness

Holy Madness

Sacred Paths

Wholeness or Transcendence?

The Philosophy of Classical Yoga

Introduction to the Bhagavad-Gita

Living Yoga (with Stephan Bodian)

Shambhala Encyclopedia of Yoga

Shambhala Guide to Yoga

Sacred Sexuality

Spirituality by the Numbers

In Search of the Cradle of Civilization
(with Subhash Kak and David Frawley)

THE YOGA-SŪTRA OF PATAÑJALI

A New Translation and Commentary

Georg Feuerstein

INNER TRADITIONS INTERNATIONAL
ROCHESTER, VERMONT

Inner Traditions International
One Park Street
Rochester, Vermont 05767
www.InnerTraditions.com

Respectfully dedicated to Mahārṣi Patañjali

LIBRARY OF CONGRESS CATALOGING-IN-PUBLICATION DATA
Patañjali.
[Yogasūtra. English]
The Yoga-sutra of Patanjali : a new translation and commentary / Georg Feuerstein.
p. cm.
Translation of: Yogasūtra.
Reprint. Originally published: Folkestone, Eng. : Dawson, 1979.
Includes bibliographical references.
ISBN 978-0-89281-262-2
ISBN 0-89281-262-1 :
1. Yoga—Early works to 1800. 2. Patañjali. Yogasūtra.
I. Feuerstein, Georg. II. Title.
B132.Y6P267 1989
181'.452—dc20 89-38375
CIP

Printed and bound in the United States

20 19 18 17

CONTENTS

Some men refuse to recognize the depth of something because they demand that the profound should manifest itself in the same way as the superficial.

A. T. de Nicolás, *Avatāra* (p.8)

PREFACE TO THE AMERICAN EDITION

Yoga comprises so many different approaches and schools that one is justified in calling it the most versatile spiritual tradition in the world. This is not really surprising considering that it has a history of possibly more than 4,000 years. I have outlined the fascinating evolution of yogic ideas and practices in some detail in my book *Yoga: The Technology of Ecstasy.*

The present volume focuses on one specific branch of the tree of Yoga—the philosophical school of Patañjali, known as the "Royal Yoga" (*rāja-yoga*) or "Yoga system" (*yoga-darśana*). In particular, I am offering here a word-by-word rendering of Patañjali's aphorisms on Yoga, the *Yoga-Sūtra.* I have been pondering this short Sanskrit work for the past twenty-five years, and I am convinced it contains enough enigmas to continue to intrigue me for the next quarter of a century.

I believe that every student of Yoga should not only read but actually study the *Yoga-Sūtra.* It is an excellent way of delving into the metaphysics *and* the spiritual practice of Yoga. All too often, Western students want to bypass the philosophical aspects of Yoga and get on with its practice. But it is impossible to practice Yoga authentically without first having grasped its metaphysics. Conversely, Yoga metaphysics will not reveal its full depth to someone who stays aloof from the practical disciplines. There is another side to this, and that is the fact that study (*svādhyāya*) is an excellent way of disciplining the mind and of deepening one's self-knowledge. It is no accident that many yogic schools insist that the student should enrich his or her spiritual life through careful study of the sacred scriptures.

The *Yoga-Sūtra* offers a wonderful opportunity to expose oneself to the condensed wisdom of centuries of spiritual experimentation and to allow one of the great adepts of that tradition to inspire one's personal practice of Yoga.

I am grateful to Ehud C. Sperling, president of Inner Traditions International, for making this translation of the *Yoga-Sūtra* available again to spiritual practitioners around the world. It seems only fitting to dedicate this book to the one person who has inspired me the most during my long sojourn through yogic territory—Mahārṣi Patañjali.

Georg Feuerstein

PREFACE TO THE ORIGINAL EDITION

As with my *Textbook of Yoga*, the present volume was also written in direct response to the request of a number of students of Yoga. Although there is no dearth of readily available popular renderings of the *Yoga-Sūtra* of Patañjali, many of the more serious practitioners seem to question the credibility of most of these translations. As they expressed to me in conversation and in their letters, what they needed to pursue their individual or group studies was an unadulterated translation of this important and profound Yoga text, based on the insights of critical scholarship but without the specialist's overwhelming apparatus of philological and historical or philosophical glosses.

Having myself waded through the flood of so-called translations, many of which cannot possibly claim to be more than highly subjective paraphrases, I have always sympathised with those who desired a more authentic rendering. However, my professional commitments and other obligations prevented me until recently from meeting this demand for a new, and I hope more useful, translation of this grand Yoga classic.

My study of the *Yoga-Sūtra* dates back well over ten years, and I remember having first translated Patañjali's treatise in 1964 into German. A couple of years later I prepared an English translation mainly for my own personal consumption. As my research on

Yoga—especially Classical Yoga—made progress, this original version was gradually superseded by an improved, critical translation which I now offer and dedicate to the growing circle of serious students of Yoga. I do so, however, in full awareness of the fact that there can never be any finality in one's knowledge and understanding of the knowable universe, least of all those aspects of it which belong to the realm of human culture. This is particularly true of historical realities (such as philosophical systems) which, in addition, are part of a civilisation other than one's own. Every translation is willy-nilly an interpretation—an approximation which can always be improved upon. Such strictures are even more pertinent in regard to a text which was composed roughly two thousand years ago by an unknown author in a difficult language, and which presents in no more than 195 Sanskrit aphorisms the 'bones' of a highly complicated thought structure which, in turn, is rooted in an incredibly vast and, to us, alien cultural universe, namely the Indian civilisation.

To place this problem which every translator faces into a larger context, I wish to remind the reader that *all* knowledge is interpretative. There are no *hard* facts, and *pure* objectivity is a myth. The reality which we perceive is always *our* reality, and what we call 'facts' are properly speaking events which we, as we become conscious of them, immediately interpret in terms of our specific cultural and personal patterns of thought and experience. This is precisely why so many scholars in the past have completely failed to understand Yoga. For, according to the system of thought (or, rather, 'belief system') subscribed to by the overriding majority of twentieth-century scientists, the world of 'inner space' with which Yoga deals, is not worth any investigation and, practically, does not even exist.

I have often criticised this fatal attitude, which is tantamount to an outright denial of a whole dimension of human experience. It is not only negative and dull, but has long been condemned as false by the sciences themselves. But scientists are human, and like most human beings they find it difficult and painful to abandon cherished ideas and attitudes even if these have been shown to be untenable in the light of scientific knowledge. This, too, is part of our individual process of interpreting the world. Because we do not know the things as they are in themselves, but construct so to speak the reality we experience, we are free to exclude, repress or misinterpret certain facts which would otherwise prove extremely irksome and perhaps challenge the very foundation of our personal philosophy of life.

The history of Yoga research offers ample examples of what happens when two different conceptual worlds become confronted; that of the scholar whose entire socialisation and education makes him inclined to close his eyes to the 'invisible' reality of consciousness, and the *yogin*'s world which is the bottomless one of psyche and mind. Fortunately, in recent years a somewhat less infelicitous and perhaps more appreciative attitude towards Indian philosophy and Yoga has made headway in scholarly circles. I wish to quote a recent statement, characteristic of this happy tendency, by a Jesuit fellow-translator of the *Yoga-Sūtra*, who with exceptional frankness declares his admiration for Patañjali's work thus:

> The technique of stilling and voiding the mind, so as to make it square with the pure undetermined Awareness-light . . . is a magnificent masterpiece. The undeniable interactions of purely somatic dispositions and of ethical conduct with man's psychical states, and the influence of these on our process of knowledge, have been keenly observed by the yogis whose experiences Patañjali has marvellously synthesized . . . It is to the credit of *Pātañjala Yoga* to have discarded all forms of extremism . . . It strikes a harmonious balance between all the constituent factors of human values and, without doing violence to our human psychosis, without irritating it, without breaking up our psychical selves, it serenely induces an internal dissolution of our human personality . . . Though the technique of *Pātañjala Yoga* is a gentle method, it requires a tremendous will power, not that ardent effort which men can muster for some short time, as when one is facing martyrdom, but rather an untiring and relentless tenacity of purpose and unflinching determination.*

To return to the question of the difficulties which confront the translator of such a text as the *Yoga-Sūtra*, it is vital that the reader should appreciate the fact that Patañjali's work is a technical treatise on Yoga and not a popular compendium or digest. Where this all-important fact is ignored, deliberately or otherwise, the translator will achieve nothing but a diluted version which is bound to be both naive and distorted. The majority of renderings on the market today bear witness to this. Being a work of a technical nature, the *Yoga-Sūtra* also employs a technical language. Therefore it would be entirely unsatisfactory to use our everyday vocabulary to express complex concepts for which the author himself had to find special Sanskrit terms. Hence the reader, if his interest in reaching a sound understanding of the original is genuine, must meet the translator half way. In other words, he must be prepared to bear with him when he introduces technical terms, borrowed from philosophy or psychology, to express the philosophical or psychological concepts of the Sanskrit original.

* G. M. Koelman (1970), pp. 255–6.

I have occasionally been reproached by students for using such 'monstrous' words as 'presented-idea' (for *pratyaya*) or 'enstasy' (for *samādhi*) when 'thought' or 'ecstasy' would do just as well. I hope that my insistence on utilising special terms for concepts of a decidedly technical nature will be found congenial as the reader works through this translation. I trust that he will gradually realise that the apparent awkwardness of such terms as the above-mentioned is redeemed by their inherent usefulness in terms of precision and ultimate clarity.

To enter a new conceptual world always means to learn a new language. For example, for our purposes it suffices to call the one-humped beast of burden found throughout the Middle East a dromedary. But for the desert nomads, who depend on the dromedary for transport, food, milk, clothing, shelter and medicine, a far more differentiated vocabulary is necessary, and we find that they employ scores of words to refer to the same species. If we wanted to comprehend the 'world' inhabited by these nomads, we would perforce have to acquire a whole range of new concepts, and to find (or create where necessary) new words to be able to express them in our own language.

It is fraught with difficulty to give hackneyed expressions, all of a sudden, a sharply delimited meaning. For instance, the Sanskrit word *īśvara* has often been rendered by the familiar and nowadays totally ambiguous word 'god'. However, the concept 'god' has far too many definite associations for us ever adequately to reflect the Sanskrit concept of *īśvara*. Thus 'the lord' is neither the creator, upholder or destroyer of the universe, nor is he judge over good and evil, right and wrong, nor supreme arbiter of human fates. To attribute therefore such qualities or functions to *īśvara* would be a severe misconstruction of the concept as intended by Patañjali.

It is part of the translator's task to remain constantly vigilant lest he project into the original what is not there. Projection, of course, is an all too human pastime, and a good deal of the scientific enterprise has to do with identifying and removing such projections. To what degree I have succeeded in withholding premature judgement and in letting the text speak for itself, future research on the *Yoga-Sūtra* will no doubt evince. As I have observed above, there is no finality in the knowledge process, and a text like the *Yoga-Sūtra* has too much depth to be fathomed out in one attempt, or possibly even in one hundred attempts. The great German indologist and philosopher Paul Deussen used to make the *sūtras* the subject of his meditations, and apparently so did the other celebrated orientalist Max Müller. How many more generations of thoughtful students of

Yoga can Patañjali's work inspire! It is still the best gateway to the whole, many-faceted phenomenon of Yoga.

In this book I propose to do no more than guide the reader to the essentials of Patañjali's Yoga. I make no pretence to an exhaustive portrayal of his philosophy or complete analysis of the *Yoga-Sūtra*. My translation and the brief exegetical notes thereon are based on extensive textual and semantic studies, but I am aware that there are still many aspects which I have not yet touched upon or understood. In view of the fact that not a few of the readers will want to use this translation for more than a cursory reading, I thought it best to prefix my rendering with the transliterated Sanskrit text (based on the Benares edition) and a word-by-word translation. This procedure will enable those geared towards a deeper study of the text to check up on this and other English versions. Even though the *Yoga-Sūtra* is not a manual containing concrete instructions about the actual practice of Yoga, nonetheless the attentive reader is bound to find a wealth of hints and ideas which will enrich his personal practice greatly.

Sanskrit is a notoriously concise language. This fact increases the difficulty of the translator's task. In addition, Patañjali employs a particular style of writing which became prominent about two millennia ago. In the *sūtra*-style the syntactical requirements are reduced to their barest minimum. This leads to half-sentences which basically are only a string of nouns and adjectives without auxiliary verbs or verbs unless these are absolutely essential. This extreme terseness cannot be imitated successfully in English which requires more 'flesh' on the 'bones' to make sense. For example, the second aphorism of the *Yoga-Sūtra* is a concatenation of merely four words (*viz. yogaś-citta-vṛtti-nirodhaḥ*), but in English nine words are required to clarify the relationship pertaining between these terms (*viz.* 'Yoga is the restriction of the fluctuations of consciousness'). In Sanskrit the same clarifying function is fulfilled by the positioning of the words and the use of the proper case endings, e.g. *yogaś* (= *yogaḥ*) and *nirodhaḥ*. This double nominative indicates equivalence, that is, 'Yoga equals restriction of . . .'. But I will not go into these linguistic details further. For those who wish to learn Sanskrit, there is now available a good self-teacher compiled with much dedication by the late Professor Michael Coulson and published in the *Teach Yourself Series* (see bibliography).

Scientific knowledge is an accumulative process, and every researcher stands on the shoulders of his predecessors. With regard to the present piece of work, I am under particular obligation to several formidable scholars, especially Professors J. W. Hauer, M.

Eliade, C. Pensa and S. Dasgupta. I have also benefited from the largely accurate translation by Professor J. H. Woods, published more than sixty years ago as volume XVII of the *Harvard Oriental Series*. When one, in addition, opts for an integrative approach, as I have done in the past, this indebtedness is multiplied a hundredfold, extending to large numbers of scholars outside one's own discipline.

To illustrate what I mean: research on Classical Yoga is but a special domain within Yoga research in general; this again is embedded in the study of Indian soteriology (liberation teachings), which in turn is part of the pool of general indology. Yet this pool is not isolated either. There are many tributaries which an integrative approach must consider, such as comparative civilisations, psychohistory, comparative methodology, hermeneutics, philosophy, history of religions, transpersonal psychology, parapsychology, psychosomatic medicine, etc. Needless to say, no one person can master all these disciplines, or have more than a very general grasp of them. But this is also unnecessary. It suffices to have a fair comprehension of those aspects of this formidable array of disciplines which are immediately relevant to research on Yoga. Understandably, this kind of integrative approach is not widely practised, for few are willing to risk failure and ridicule. However, it always seemed to me that the study of Yoga is singularly suited, and in fact demands, such a broadly based approach. It presents to the researcher the unique challenge of overcoming, in a small but important area of enquiry, the fragmentation of knowledge symptomatic of the age we live in. I think that this is well worth any possible reprimands which other specialists may feel called upon to make. It is my unwavering conviction that only by a determined struggle for a new, whole conception of man, and the simultaneous restoration of value and meaning to human existence, will we collectively and as individuals be able to face up to a more than precarious future. I consider as an integral part of this endeavour the establishment of a continuous dialogue between the specialist and the layman. The present book is intended as a small contribution to such a dialogue between the professional Yoga researcher and the practitioner of Yoga. I hope that my work will be found useful.

INTRODUCTION

Verily, there is no merit higher than Yoga, no good higher than Yoga, no subtlety higher than Yoga; there is nothing that is higher than Yoga.

Yogaśikhā-Upaniṣad I.67

PATAÑJALI AND THE EXEGETICAL LITERATURE

Virtually nothing is known about the author of our text: at least nothing of any degree of historical certainty. According to native learned traditions, Patañjali is allegedly identical with the famous Sanskrit grammarian of that name, who lived some time in the second century B.C. Legend, again, knows of him as the incarnation of the serpent-king Ananta, a manifestation of god Viṣṇu, who is believed to encircle the earth. This identification is at least of symbolic interest. For the serpent race over which Ananta or Śeṣa presides is associated, in mythology, with the guarding of the esoteric lore, and Yoga is of course the secret tradition *par excellence.* Other interpretations are possible, but of necessity equally unhistorical. Here we can merely register our profound ignorance about the historical personality of the author of the *Yoga-Sūtra*, and simply re-affirm the finding of earlier scholars that Patañjali the Yoga writer and his namesake the grammarian were in all probability *not* identical. The two are well separated in time by four or five centuries, for the *Yoga-Sūtra* is a product of the third century A.D.

To a western audience which is accustomed to fairly detailed biographies of its literary heroes, such anonymity is inexplicable. In India, however, it is the rule rather than the exception. Popular imagination was free to attribute such anonymous works unrestrainedly to famous writers and even perfectly mythological figures who could not possibly have anything to do with their composition. For instance, a certain Vyāsa (the name means literally 'collator') is said to have compiled the Vedas and composed not only the great national epic including its most celebrated tract, the *Bhagavad-Gītā*, but also the voluminous Purāṇa-literature and, not least, the oldest and single most important commentary on the *Yoga-Sūtra*, the *Bhāṣya*.

Whatever the real name of the author of the *Yoga-Bhāṣya* may have been, it is improbable that he was a protagonist of Patañjali's school of Yoga. There is reason to believe that he in fact belonged to a particular Sāṃkhya school. As one might expect, his knowledge of the Yoga system as outlined in the aphorisms is that of an empathetic *outsider*—and this appears to be the case with all the other exegetes as well. None of the extant Sanskrit commentaries can be said to be by a proponent of Patañjali's school. This raises the question whether Patañjali actually instituted such a school, or whether he was just a maverick *yogin* who, besides composing the aphorisms, engaged in no teaching whatsoever, thus leaving no pupils behind to carry on the tradition of his intellectually consolidated Yoga. The second alternative strikes one as incredible. First of all, Patañjali must have been a sufficiently important figure within the Yoga tradition at large even to consider producing an authoritative aphoristic digest, which means that he also must have had hosts of pupils eager to learn from him. Secondly, it would also seem quite unlikely that among all these adherents there was not one to continue the tradition. In point of fact, Svāmī Hariharānanda Āraṇya (1869–1947), author of a recent Sanskrit commentary on the *Yoga-Sūtra*, claimed that his teacher, Svāmī Trilokī Āraṇya, was a distinguished member of the line of Yoga *gurus* established by Patañjali. Considering that Svāmī Hariharānanda's exegesis does not bring anything really new, it seems doubtful that the oral tradition of his particular *paraṃparā* or line of succession has preserved any additional knowledge with regard to the theoretical framework of Classical Yoga.

There is always the slight possibility that somewhere in one of the Indian libraries, among literally thousands of hitherto unread manuscripts, there may still be a copy of a Sanskrit commentary which was written by a disciple of Patañjali. On the other hand, there may never have been such a work at all, which would have prompted scholars from non-yogic traditions, like Vyāsa or Vācaspati Miśra, to compose more or less authentic commentaries on the *Yoga-Sūtra*.

As the oldest commentary, the *Yoga-Bhāṣya* provides the key to all other exegeses. More than any of the later commentators, Vyāsa appears to have been fairly familiar with the practical aspects of Yoga, which prompted at least one scholar, J. W. Hauer (1958), to see in him a practising *Yogin* (though with a distinct Sāṃkhya background). Possibly the most academic exegete is Vācaspati Miśra, a ninth-century pundit who wrote brilliant works on Sāṃkhya and Vedānta philosophy and other schools of thought. Two centuries later, King Bhoja wrote a commentary entitled *Rāja-Mārtaṇḍa* which was largely inspired by Vyāsa's and Vācaspati Miśra's exegetical efforts. Vijñāna Bhikṣu, again, was a philosopher of distinction who, apart from numerous expositional works of great originality, also wrote a detailed commentary to the *Yoga-Sūtra*, the so-called *Yoga-Vārttika*, and an abstract of this huge scholium, the *Yoga-Sāra-Saṃgraha*. Other interpreters and exegetes followed, displaying varying degrees of insight and originality, though more often than not obscuring rather than illuminating the complex world of ideas so pithily portrayed in the aphorisms of Patañjali.

Reading and re-reading the *Yoga-Sūtra*, one soon begins to piece together a mental image, or profile, quite hypothetical, of its author. It is the picture of a systematic thinker with a traditional bend of mind, a practical metaphysician who is lucid and precise in his formulations, not over-anxious to enter into polemics with other schools and obviously well-established in the *practice* of Yoga. His work is remarkable for its dispassionate temper. This cannot be accounted for by the extreme terseness of his aphoristic style alone. After all, Pascal succeeded in communicating powerful emotive images by the same method. Rather, the conspicuous absence of all emotionality from the *Yoga-Sūtra* must be explained by the author's other-worldly philosophy and his personal character which is that of a genuine renunciant and *yogin*.

Patañjali is visible proof for the fact that mysticism *can* be approached rationally and that, equally importantly, contemplative interests and intellectual pursuits *can* be fruitfully combined in one person. This lesson is not new, for it has long been taught within the context of Christianity by such outstanding theologians and mystics as St Augustine and Meister Eckehart. They, together with Patañjali, demonstrate a further truth, namely that the cultivation of mystical inwardness is not, in principle, incompatible with the Establishment—a particularly relevant observation at a time when mysticism tends to be mingled with social protest and even militancy.

SOME PHILOSOPHICAL CONCEPTS OF KRIYĀ-YOGA

As I wish to avoid unnecessary overlap with the material presented in my *The Essence of Yoga*, I will confine myself in the following to a brief sketch of the cardinal points of Patañjali's 'philosophy'. Those who are new to, or in need of a refresher about, the history, literature, and major schools of Yoga, are best advised to read through *Yoga: The Technology of Ecstasy* for the necessary background information.

The 'philosophy' expounded in the *Yoga-Sūtra* is, strictly speaking, more than what is commonly understood by that term. It is not merely a system of logically related propositions dealing with the meaning of reality in its entirety (which is one possible definition of philosophy). It contains also strong ethical prescriptions and, above all, includes a method for the systematic transformation of consciousness with the ultimate purpose of achieving 'liberation' or 'Self realisation', postulated by Yoga ethics as the highest good. These various aspects cannot be separated from each other, except for analytical purposes in order to understand better how the whole system hangs together.

Philosophy as an exercise in purely abstract thinking which remains without consequence in daily life is not something Patañjali or any other *yogin* would subscribe to. Their conception of philosophy is perhaps more akin to the kind of broad-minded enquiry which 'love of wisdom' originally stood for. Still the 'wisdom' (*sophía*) sought after in Yoga goes beyond the sort of inspired understanding Socrates and his pupils strove for. Patañjali is concerned with the very source or possibility of all knowledge, namely the *root-consciousness* which he calls *puruṣa*, *draṣṭṛ*, *citi-śakti* and *svāmin*. This is admittedly a difficult concept to grasp and one which has vexed a number of western psychologists and philosophers of the recent past, to mention only William James, C. G. Jung and J.-P. Sartre. Some have rejected it as useless or fictitious, others have tried to make sense of it by re-interpreting it, and a few have confessed their complete bafflement. This is not the place to re-examine all the various pros and cons raised by these thinkers. What we are concerned with is to understand what this concept means in the context of Patañjali's thought.

Here one all-important fact must be borne in mind, namely that this key concept in Yoga is not the product of mere abstract speculation as is, for instance, the notion of a 'non-distributive lattice' developed by logicians. Rather the concept of *puruṣa* was formulated in order to explain a certain kind of experience, or experienced reality, encountered at the apex of the yogic process of interiorisation. It is thus a concept which has a concrete referent. Any other interpretation not only runs counter to the explanation given by the *yogins* themselves, but is also convergent with the superficial opinion which reduces yogic experiences to hallucinations or, at best, mere brain functions. The question, therefore, is not really whether the yogic *puruṣa* is real or imaginary, but rather whether or not the conceptualisation of whatever experience the concept stands for is adequate, or, to put it differently, what kind of experience the concept is supposed to capture. The reason why I am not prepared even to consider the possibility that it simply represents a meaningless word, as any hard-headed positivist is apt to claim, is that this would force me to deny, without sufficient reason, the validity of the testimony of thousands of individuals of different ages and countries, and thereby to dump a significant part of the total human experience on to the garbage heap. Especially in our epoch, where much of our feeling, thinking and behaviour has already been 'frozen' around a few narrow themes—sex, status, work as drudgery, passive spectatorship, etc.—it would be mindless to avow any reductionist view which seeks to explain away an experience that clearly challenges the very basis of the contemporary life style and that could be instrumental in restoring a more adequate conception of man.

If *puruṣa* is not just an empty concept but the symbol of an experience, which has as its content something real and not imaginary, we ere led to consider the question of the fit between the concept and the reality it is intended to express. More specifically, we must ask ourselves whether the experience labelled '*puruṣa*' is identical with the experience labelled '*puruṣa*' in Sāṃkhya thought, '*ātman*' or '*brahman*' in Vedānta, '*nirvāṇa*' in Buddhism or 'God' in Christian mysticism. Those who believe in the transcendental unity of transpersonal experiencing are emphatic that all these designations refer to one and the same reality, and that they are variations of basically the same experience. They explain the different terms and the concepts they stand for as the result of the philosophical bias or linguistic preferences of those who formulated them. This explanation is too simplistic. It fails to explain why the descriptions of a supposedly uniform experience often differ considerably from each other. This fact remains unintelligible unless one assumes that there is not one single experience, labelled differently, but several distinct experiences with a number of features in common. That this is not just western sophistry is evident from the fact that this problem has been recognised long ago by the Indian thinkers themselves.

It has also occasionally been suggested that although the reality underlying these top-level experiences is the same in each case, it is due to the individual capacity of the *yogin, vedāntin* or mystic that it is conceptualised in such a variety of ways. Not infrequently one school puts its goal above all others arguing that either it represents a higher experience or a better conceptualisation than those given out by the rival schools. An analogy taken from western scientific thinking may help us to understand this phenomenon. Before Copernicus, millions of people conceptualised the earth as a flat disc over which arched the celestial vault. Copernicus conceptualised it as a sphere rolling in eternal grooves around the sun. Today we know (i.e. conceptualise) the globe as a geoid (a somewhat imperfect sphere) speeding along in empty (or near-empty) space in a not quite perfect trajectory (it 'wobbles'). How tomorrow's astronomers will look at planetary mechanics no one can tell. Truth is thus the best available conceptual approximation to reality. Of course, as long as we have not ascended to the same heights as the *yogins* and mystics of East and West, we must suspend all judgement on the truth value of their explanations. We can merely comment on their inherent logical consistency, or lack of it, and consider their plausibility in the over-all context of available documentation of transpersonal experiences. It is the formidable task of future comparative research to document the great differentiation in this kind of experiencing and to work out some sort of structural framework within which all these varied experiences can find a place.

But to return to Patañjali's philosophy. He makes two fundamental assertions about *puruṣa*. The first is that the *puruṣa* is overwhelmingly *real*, that it is in fact more real than anything encountered in ordinary experience. The second claim is that it is the essential nature of man and as such is the most worthy object of all human motivation. These two suppositions—the *ontological* claim of the supreme reality of *puruṣa* and the *axiological* claim about its utmost valority—are inseparable. *Puruṣa* is supreme value, the *summum bonum*, precisely because it (or he) is the highest reality or, more accurately, is experienced as the highest reality, and *vice versa*.

Essentially the same idea is found in the other philosophical schools (*darśana*). In some Vedānta texts, the *ātman* (corresponding, though not identical with the *puruṣa*) is actually referred to as *niḥśreyasa* or 'the highest good'. As one scholar put it succinctly, in the soteriological traditions of India 'the ultimate concern of man is man'[1]. This is to say, the highest goal to which man can, and ought to, aspire does not lie in the outer world but within himself, in his core being. But how can man make himself the object of his motivation? Does this not amount to absolute egotism? To answer this question from the viewpoint of Classical Yoga—and other answers are possible!—Patañjali would not deny the egotistic element contained in his prescription to realise the Self or root-consciousness. All living beings perpetuate their own life by feeding on the life of others, both in a metaphorical and a literal sense. The will to live (*abhiniveśa*), Patañjali observes (II.9), is rooted even in the sage who has turned his heart and mind away from worldly things, nay from life as such. The *yogin's* struggle to discover his true Self can not therefore be devoid of all selfishness. Naturally, there is a vast difference between the egotism displayed, say, in the greed for power or sensation, and the egotism entailed in the yogic endeavour once and for all to step out of this vicious circle. Egotism is killed at its roots once the Self is realised. The ego is something which pertains to a particular body-mind complex, but the Self is beyond space and time. Hence it is often referred to as the transcendental or 'higher' Self, as distinct from the phenomenal or 'lower' self (or ego, or personality). Possibly this unconditional injunction to realise the Self, implicit in Patañjali's philosophy, is too one-sided. Because Patañjali draws such a strict distinction between the Self and the non-self (i.e. the world), regarding the former as the ultimate value, he is forced to teach a form of emancipation which presupposes the total extinction of man as we know him.

Even if we are convinced of the reality of *puruṣa*, on what grounds

[1] F. V. Catalina (1968).

need we accept the idea that Self-realisation, as taught by Patañjali, does indeed constitute the highest value which we can aspire to? Does the realisation of this value not coincide with our extinction as beings in space and time? Why should such an ideal appeal to us? That the form of Self-realisation promoted by Patañjali is indeed of this radical type can be inferred from his very last aphorism (IV.34) which speaks of the reabsorption of the primary-constituents into the world-ground. This implies that emancipation follows upon the total dissolution of the organism, here understood to comprise both the bodily and the psycho-mental life. A more moderate version of Self-realisation or emancipation is taught in certain Vedānta schools, where a distinction is made between *jīvan-mukti* or liberation in life and *videha-mukti* or liberation upon death. The ideal of liberation in life is founded on the insight that since the realisation of the Self is anyhow an aspatial/atemporal event, the organism is not at all involved and that therefore emancipation need not be preceded by physical and mental extinction. This is a less extreme, though equally problematic, view.

Whether we consider the possibility of liberation in life or liberation after the discarding of the body, we still have to answer the initial question: why should the Self constitute the ultimate value? Why are we not asked to strive for truth, knowledge, beauty or happiness? I think all *darśanas* give an identical answer to this crucial question: the supreme value of Self-realisation lies in the fact that the Self is the only reality that will remain after everything else has been eroded and cancelled by time. This conviction is expressed in another great Yoga classic, the *Bhagavad-Gītā* (II.20) in the following words: 'Never is He born or dies. He did not come into being, nor shall He ever come to be. This primeval [Self] is unborn, eternal, everlasting. It is not slain when the body is slain.'

In contrast to the ceaselessly changing world, the Self is permanently stable. As Patañjali puts it (IV.18), the Self is the 'knower', i.e. that which is characterised by immutability (*apariṇāmitva*). It is in this unshakable stability of our inmost Self that Patañjali sees its great value as a panacea for the eradication of our anxiety-ridden human condition. Realisation of the root-consciousness means the conquest of all fear, all ills, all neuroses. But, as I have pointed out already, this conquest presupposes that we turn our back on all things of the world, on life itself. Patañjali's is not a way of living *in* the world free from fear of death or loss of any kind, but of acquiring an other-worldly dimension of existence where properly speaking it no longer makes any sense to talk of fear or its removal. The transformation of human nature as envisaged in Classical Yoga is entirely a process of negation of everything that is ordinarily considered as typically human.

Such a radical re-shaping of man—one can also call it his 'de-humanisation'—by no means appeals to everybody, and many no doubt will spontaneously reject this stance. Whatever our personal predilection may be on this issue, whether we opt for or against this kind of other-worldly liberation, we should not discard off-hand the *possibility* of either mode of liberation.

By and large, the Indian thinkers and seers have tended to regard the ideal of Self-realisation *in* life as the more desirable goal, and it seems to me that this is perhaps also philosophically more satisfactory, if only because it appears the more comprehensive and integral view of the two. If we can find our Self *and* remain active in the world for as long as we may, surely this is a more inspiring goal than simple world transcendence. It was this recognition which led to the developments in Mahāyāna-Buddhism associated with the celebrated ideal of the *bodhisattva*, the enlightened being, who willingly forgoes the privilege of liberation for the spiritual good of all other sentient beings.

Nevertheless, this does not appear to be Patañjali's position. According to him, man's true nature is the eternal Self, and his spatio-temporal existence is a mere epiphenomenon. For some ultimately inexplicable reason this pure, unchanging Self identifies itself with a particular organism. This false identification is the cause of all man's ills. The means to terminate his suffering is by way of self-absorption, by withdrawing and demolishing all pseudo-identities, until the Self is 'excavated' from all the manifold layers of psycho-mental debris.

There is an alternative to Patañjali's dualistic model which is founded on an uncompromising dichotomy between Self (or Selves) and the world. This is Ken Wilber's (1977) conception of a 'spectrum of consciousness'—an idea first formulated by the famous American pioneer of psychology, William James. In analogy with the electro-magnetic spectrum of physics, Wilber suggests that the diverse levels of consciousness as described by western and eastern psychologists (in the broadest sense of the term), can profitably be viewed as parts ('bands') of a single spectrum. 'Out of an infinite number of possible levels made available to us through the revelations of psychoanalysis, Yogacara Buddhism, Jungian analysis, Vedanta Hinduism, Gestalt therapy, Vajrayana, Psychosynthesis, and the like, three major bands . . . have been selected on the basis of their simplicity and their ease of identification.'[2] The three levels in question are what he calls the 'ego level', the 'existential level' and the 'level of Mind'. These roughly correspond with Patañjali's *citta, asmitā-mātra* and *puruṣa* respectively.

Wilber characterises the ego level (or *citta*) as 'that band of consciousness that comprises our role, our picture of ourself, our self-image, with both its conscious and unconscious [*sic*] aspects, as well as the analytical and discriminatory nature of the intellect, of our "mind"'. The second major level 'involves our total organism, our soma as well as our psyche, and thus comprises our basic sense of existence, of being, along with our cultural premises that in many ways mold this basic sensation of existence'. Finally, the third level of 'Mind', 'is commonly termed mystical consciousness, and it entails the sensation that you are fundamentally one with the universe'. Thus instead of defining human nature in terms of 'Mind' only, as does Patañjali, this spectrum model operates with a conception of man that includes the entire range of modes of existence or cognition open to him. Wilber, moreover, shows how the various eastern and western psychological disciplines address specific 'bands' or 'frequencies' of the consciousness spectrum. Misunderstanding and confusion arise when the methods and logic appropriate to one 'band' are applied to another level, such as when psychoanalysts try to explain the *root-consciousness* in terms of the unconscious (a dubious concept in itself), or when advocates of eastern paths condemn the western psychologists' endeavours to create *merely* a healthy ego or a socially viable personality.

This metaphor of the spectrum of consciousness brings to our mind the vast potential of human existence. We can either become congealed on one particular level, or we can broaden out and learn to master other sectors of this enormous keyboard, to explore the different dimensions of reality, or at least open ourselves to them. William James observed more than seven decades ago that 'the world of our present consciousness is only one out of many worlds of consciouness that exist, and that those other worlds must contain experiences which have a meaning for our life also'.[3]

One final point with regard to the problem of Self in Classical Yoga must be made. This concerns the doctrine of the plurality of transcendental Selves allegedly subscribed to by Patañjali. Unlike Vedānta, which recognises but a single Self (the *ātman*) for all beings, Classical Yoga is well-known for its teaching that every

[2] K. Wilber (1977), p. 18.
[3] Quoted in op. cit., p. 24.

being has its own Self. In fact, there is not a single reference in the *Yoga-Sūtra* to the effect that there is a multiplicity of *puruṣas*. However, Vyāsa and the other exegetes could be right in ascribing this doctrine to Patañjali, for it would be in keeping with his dualist philosophy. Nevertheless, since the *puruṣa* represents an entity of sorts, abiding beyond space and time and being both omnipresent and omniscient, the question of the Self's singularity or plurality is a largely academic one.

So far I have dealt mainly with Patañjali's most significant concept, that of the root-consciousness or Self. Next I intend to focus briefly on the second mainstay of his philosophy, *viz.* his concept of 'nature' or *prakṛti.* This term denotes everything the Self is not, namely the *entire* cosmos—from the physical objects to the psychic and mental realities. In contradistinction to the Self, which is pure subjectivity, *prakṛti* represents objective reality. It is that which is apperceived by the Self. Patañjali also calls it 'the owned' (*sva*, II.23), 'the seen' (*dṛṣṭa*, II.17) and 'the grasped' (*grāhya*, I.41). Like the Self, the world in its entirety is absolutely real. Patañjali rejects the notion that it is a mere thought product or imaginary projection by the Self, but firmly maintains that it exists in its own right. Idealism is explicitly refuted in aphorism IV.16.

Whereas the Self is unruffled awareness, root-consciousness, the world-ground and its products are essentially *unconscious*. However, this dichotomy between Self and world is not quite the same as the Cartesian dualism between *res cogitans* and *res extensa*. For Patañjali includes among the latter category, i.e. *prakṛti*, also the psyche and mind. Were it not for the illuminating power of the Self, the psycho-mental complex would forever lack any sign of conscious activity. Consciousness, that is consciousness-of-something, is in a way the product of the combined presence of Self and non-self (see IV.17ff.).

The concepts of *puruṣa* and *prakṛti* belong to the oldest stock of Indian metaphysical thought. The term *prakṛti* is found already in the *Atharvaveda* and was, like its counterpart *puruṣa*, intimately connected with the development of the early Yoga-Sāṃkhya tradition. Both Yoga and Sāṃkhya use this technical term to designate nature in its undifferentiated, transcendental state *and* its differentiated, multiform condition. This conception is no more abstract than the modern notion of a space-time continuum, and in fact one can discover many interesting similarities between both formulations. The surprising likeness which exists between the archaic cosmogonic model of Yoga and its contemporary equivalent, as espoused by modern cosmology and nuclear physics, has often been remarked upon though still awaits a satisfactory explanation.

Patañjali, as is rarely noticed, employs the word *prakṛti* in the singular and, on one occasion (IV.3), in the plural. Historically, this can be explained on the basis of the antecedent developments of 'epic' Yoga and Sāṃkhya as recorded, above all, in the *Mahābhārata*. Logically, this double usage is justified by the twin nature of *prakṛti* itself. It is both single and multiple, potentiality and actuality. In its transcendental aspect, as the core of all objectively existing things, it is uniform—we would perhaps say an undifferentiated energy field. In its phenomenal aspect, on the other hand, it is the multiplex cosmos evolved from the world-ground in clearly discernible evolutionary stages.

As *prakṛti*

> unrolls itself it manifests the multidimensional structure of the universe. The hierarchic arrangement of the cosmos suggests comparison with a pyramid. The key-stone at the very top of the pyramid represents the unitary world-ground, its base is the realm of the particularised material objects, and the layers of brickwork in between symbolise the various categories of psychomental life, that is, the 'invisible' or 'spiritual' dimension of the universe.[4]

The way in which the manifold emerges from the One has been the special domain of enquiry of Yoga and Sāṃkhya ontology. In the various schools of these two great traditions, a good many cosmogenetic models have been elaborated, which are, on the whole, fairly similar to each other. Contrary to general opinion, I regard these models not so much as purely speculative constructions, but as a mixture of *a priori* theorising and *a posteriori* explanation of concrete yogic experiences. These models are used by the *yogin* to orient himself on his inward odyssey. They are primarily practical *maps* for the process of involution, and secondarily descriptive accounts of the gigantic process of cosmic evolution.

Over a hundred years ago, H. T. Colebrooke, who was one of the first orientalists to pay any attention to Yoga, argued that the philosophy of nature propounded in Yoga is that of the Classical Sāṃkhya—an infelicitous assumption which even a whole century of research seems to have failed to amend. The fact is that Patañjali's cosmogonic model has not only *not* been adopted lock, stock and barrel from the Sāṃkhya of Īśvara Kṛṣṇa, but is a quite self-reliant formulation which, moreover, is more appealing theoretically than its Sāṃkhya duplicate. The latter has lost much of the

[4] G. Feuerstein (1974), p. 102.

map character spoken of above, and has been turned into a rather formalistic structure. This difference is to be explained by the fact that Classical Sāṃkhya has moved away from yogic experimentation which was still part and parcel of the epic Sāṃkhya schools, and developed a strong rationalistic bias where speculation takes the place once assigned to experience.

What, then, is the particular cosmogenetic schema taught by Patañjali? In broad outline, the *Yoga-Sūtra* distinguishes, in quite unique fashion, between four major phases or levels (*parvan*) of existence:

(1) *aliṅga* (the Undifferentiate): the transcendental core of the world which is a state of sheer potentiality, also called *pradhāna* (lit. 'foundation');
(2) *liṅga-mātra* (the Differentiate): the first actualisation of the world-ground;
(3) *aviśeṣa* (the Unparticularised): the secondary actualisation, emerging out of the Differentiate, and comprising the categories of *asmitā-mātra* (the principle of individuation) and the five *tanmātras* (the sensory potentials, e.g. sound, sight, hearing, etc.);
(4) *viśeṣa* (the Particularised): the tertiary actualisation, evolving from the Unparticularised, and comprising the categories of *manas* (intellect), the ten sense-organs (*indriya*) and the five material elements (*bhūta*), viz. ether, air, fire, water and earth.

Whereas the first three levels constitute the 'subtle' (*sūkṣma*) dimension of nature, the last level is our day-to-day empirical reality. The exact interrelation between these four strata will be discussed in the comments to the relevant aphorisms. The dynamics of cosmic evolution or creation is provided by the tension inherent in the unmanifest core of the world, which can be visualised as a vast universal energy field structured by three distinct power potentials, the well-known *guṇas*.

Just as we are prone nowadays to reduce all phenomena analytically to atoms, so also the *yogin* considers the whole universe as the manifestation of the three classes of forces which make up the energy field of *prakṛti*. Although the insights of modern nuclear physics can help us to understand better this difficult yogic notion, it would nevertheless be misleading to equate, as some writers have done, the *guṇas* with our atoms or any sub-atomic particles. These two concepts are analogous, not homologous. Another common mistake is to regard the *guṇas* as 'ingredients' or 'parts' of *prakṛti* Since they are clearly said to constitute even *aliṅga* (see II.19), they must themselves be impartite. The *guṇas are prakṛti.*

The multitude of phenomena, whether they belong to the subtle dimension or the visible realm of nature, are understood as real transformations (*pariṇāma*) of one and the same first principle which lies beyond the known universe woven by space and time. This view has the technical name of *prakṛti-pariṇāma-vāda.* It entails a particular theory of causation, according to which the effect is pre-existent in its cause, also known as the *sat-kārya* doctrine, which has its modern parallel in recent thinking about potentiality and deep structures.

The present portrayal of Patañjali's philosophy would be incomplete without reference to the third major principle of his ontology, the concept of *īśvara* or 'lord'. As I have pointed out in the Preface, the word *īśvara* has time and again been misconstrued to mean 'God'. Yet it is perfectly clear from the *Yoga-Sūtra* that the *īśvara* is neither the kind of Absolute envisaged by the Vedānta thinkers, nor the anthropomorphic deity of Christianity or Judaism; nor is 'the lord' a type of enlightened super-being such as the *buddhas* or transcendental *bodhisattvas* of Hīnayāna and Mahāyāna-Buddhism respectively. Patañjali simply defines the *īśvara* as 'a special Self' (I.24) who, in contrast to the human transcendental Self, has never been involved in the mechanisms of *prakṛti*. In other words, he is that Self who at no time has foregone his perfect Self-awareness, who has never suffered the limitations of a finite consciousness. In the pre-classical schools of Yoga, the *īśvara* was still considered as the supreme entity from which emanated the whole cosmos including all the transcendental Selves. Patañjali has frequently been criticised for his diluted concept of *īśvara*. Why did he retain it at all? It is difficult to accept the idea that he should have continued to use this concept simply for historical reasons, or in order to make his philosophy acceptable to the orthodox Hindu. Considering the distinctly pragmatic tenor of his Yoga, such an allegation would appear to be preposterous.

It is preferable to assume that the *īśvara*, like the *puruṣa* and like many other concepts, stands in fact for a certain class of experiences. This would explain why this concept is of primarily *practical* significance. In aphorism I.26, the lord is styled the 'teacher of the former *yogins*'. Since the *īśvara* is by definition a transcendental principle this statement must obviously be taken metaphorically. The lord cannot possibly be thought of as becoming incarnate in order to teach those who aspire to reach Self-awareness. His instruction, therefore, must be other than active teaching: he 'guides' the *yogin* by his mere existence. This subtle and important point has been correctly understood by Mircea Eliade (1969^2) who, in unashamedly non-positivistic language, speaks of the 'metaphysical sympathy' between the lord and the inmost nucleus of man, the Self.

To conclude this précis, I wish to make some final observations about the methodological aspect of Classical Yoga. Patañjali's Yoga has usually been typified as *aṣṭa-aṅga-yoga* or the 'eightfold path' (lit. 'Yoga of eight members'). The *aṅgas* referred to are, of course, the well-known series of *yama* (general ethical principles), *niyama* (special principles of self-restraint), *āsana* (appropriate postures for meditative-absorption), *prāṇāyama* (breathing techniques), *pratyāhāra* (sense-withdrawal), *dhāraṇā* (concentration), *dhyāna* (meditative-absorption) and *samādhi* (enstasy). These are indeed discussed at some length in the *Yoga-Sūtra*. However, as I have been able to demonstrate, the particular section in which *aṣṭa-aṅga-yoga* is dealt with has a subordinate position in Patañjali's work and that the proper designation of his system is *kriyā-yoga* (as mentioned in II.1).[5] In all probability, the *aṣṭa-aṅga* section is merely a quotation or, less likely, a later interpolation. It is curious that Patañjali's Yoga should have become so exclusively associated with the idea of the eight limbs or members, but the main reason for this lies undoubtedly in the fact that the practical side of his Yoga has always attracted greater attention than the philosophy upon which it is built. This is regrettable, first, because in his Yoga, theory and practice are closely tied together so that the one makes no sense without the other, and secondly because his philosophical edifice contains many interesting issues which are well worth a deeper study.

[5] See G. Feuerstein (1979).

OVERVIEW OF TOPICS DISCUSSED BY PATAÑJALI

I.1	opening aphorism
I.2	preliminary definition of Yoga
I.3–4	the Self in relation to consciousness
I.5–11	the fluctuations of consciousness
I.12–16	the two poles of yogic interiorisation—the practice of unification and dispassion
I.17–20	types of enstasy
I.21–2	degrees of commitment
I.23–8	'the lord' and his symbolic representation
I.29–32	the obstacles on the yogic path and the means of their removal
I.33–9	specific means of steadying the consciousness fluctuations
I.40	the range of meditational objects mastered by the adept
I.41–4	types of object-oriented enstasy
I.45	definition of the concept of 'subtle' object
I.46–9	the culmination of the object-oriented enstasy
I.50	the 'seedless' enstasy
II.1–2	the three components of Kriyā-Yoga and their rationale
II.3–14	the causes-of-affliction—their nature, effects and removal
II.15–17	sorrow—its cause and removal
II.18–19	the nature of objective reality (the 'seen')
II.20–5	the nature of subjective reality (the 'seer' or Self) and its relation to the 'seen'
II.26–7	the 'vision of discernment' as the means of dispelling nescience

*II.28–9	the components and rationale of the 'eight member' Yoga
*II.30–4	specification of the constituents of 'restraint' and 'observance', and the method for ensuring their cultivation
*II.35–9	individual definitions of the various constituents of 'restraint'
*II.40–5	individual definitions of the various constituents of 'observance'
*II.46–8	the practice of 'posture' and its results
*II.49–53	the practice of 'breath control' and its results
*II.54–5	the practice of 'sense-withdrawal' and its results
*III.1	definition of 'concentration'
*III.2	definition of 'meditative-absorption'
*III.3	definition of (object-oriented) 'enstasy'
*III.4–6	definition of 'constraint' and its results
*III.7–8	explanation of what is meant by 'inner' and 'outer' members (or 'limbs') of Yoga
III.9–15	consciousness interiorisation in the light of the philosophical concept of 'transformation'
III.16–49	the practice of 'constraint' upon various contents of consciousness and the 'powers' resulting from it
III.50–1	the higher form of 'dispassion' and last possible obstacles
III.52–5	the terminal phases of interiorisation
†IV.1	the various means of obtaining the 'powers'
IV.2–5	the process of creation, with particular regard to the emergence of the finite consciousness
IV.6	the nature of consciousness transmuted through Yoga
IV.7–11	the factors underlying the mechanism of retribution and re-birth
IV.12	the nature of time
IV.13–16	further explanations about the nature of objective reality
IV.17–23	the knowledge process and the Self as ultimate principle of Awareness
IV.24	the teleological nature ('other-purposiveness') of objective reality
IV.25–8	the 'vision of discernment'
IV.29–31	the 'cloud of *dharma* enstasy' and its consequence

IV.32–4	the terminal phase of enstasy in terms of the concept of 'transformation' and liberation

Aphorisms marked * belong to the *aṣṭa-aṅga-yoga* text quoted in Patañjali's work.
The aphorism marked † is very probably a later interpolation.

ANNOTATED TRANSLATION

Translation is not simply the search for precisely equivalent ciphers or a linguistic isomorphism, but the search for a linguistic expression of another way of life.

D. W. Theobald, *An Introduction to the Philosophy of Science* (p. 135)

Perfection [in Yoga] is not achieved by wearing the apparel [of a *yogin*], or by talking about it. Practice alone is the means to success. This is the truth, without doubt.

Haṭhayoga-Pradīpikā I.66

Chapter One
SAMĀDHI-PĀDA

- This is the goal of yoga

Note: Patañjali starts his work with a series of useful definitions. The first chapter serves as an introduction, outlining the essential features of yogic practice, and hangs together so well that several previous translators have been misled into believing that it represents an entirely self-contained Yoga document. Some have gone still further and declared the section dealing with 'the lord' (*īśvara*) to be either a separate text or an interpolation. However, as I have shown in my detailed analytical study of the *Yoga-Sūtra*,[1] this text-splitting is quite unfounded.

I.1 *atha-yoga-anuśāsanam*

atha = now
yoga = lit. 'yoke/union' (from √*yuj* 'to yoke')
anuśāsana = exposition (from *anu* + √*śās* 'to instruct')

Now [commences] the exposition of Yoga.

This opening aphorism (*sūtra*) states the subject-matter and nature of Patañjali's treatise. It is clear from the use of the term 'exposition' that the *Yoga-Sūtra* is not meant to be an original philosophical tract expounding Yoga, but merely a work in which formal explanations of an already existing body of knowledge are offered. However, Patañjali is not simply a compiler but actively contributes to the elaboration of Yoga theory and philosophy, and in this respect can be said to be the founder of a particular school of Yoga, viz. Kriyā-Yoga. The mythological founder of Yoga *per se* is, according to most traditions, Hiraṇyagarbha.

[1] See G. Feuerstein (1979).

I.2 *yogaś-citta-vṛtti-nirodhaḥ*
yoga = Yoga (see I.1)
citta = consciousness (from √*cit* 'to perceive/be bright')
vṛtti = fluctuation (from √*vṛt* 'to whirl')
nirodha = restriction (from *ni* + √*rudh* 'to restrict, suppress')
Yoga is the restriction of the fluctuations of consciousness.

What is Yoga? As I have shown in my *Textbook of Yoga*, the word *yoga* has a great many meanings which range from 'yoke' to 'mathematical calculus'. However, these dictionary definitions are of little use when we search for the meaning of Yoga within the context of Indian philosophical/soteriological[2] thinking. Here Yoga stands for a particular tradition extraordinarily rich in theory and practice and by no means uniform. The Kriyā-Yoga of Patañjali, also known as Classical Yoga, is but one branch among many within this vast tradition. According to one definition, especially popular among Vedānta and Neo-Vedānta followers, Yoga means 'union'. Although this may be correct as regards certain forms of Yoga, it is definitely inapplicable to Patañjali's Kriyā-Yoga whose essence consists rather in a 'disunion', namely the disjunction of the Self (*puruṣa*) and the world (*prakṛti*). There is no question of any union with the Divine, as A. J. Bahm (1967) mistakenly assumes.

The present aphorism has generally been held to provide a definition of the nature of Patañjali's Yoga. That this is too simplistic a view becomes apparent when one carefully analyses the meaning of the three key concepts introduced here, viz. consciousness (*citta*), fluctuation (*vṛtti*) and restriction (*nirodha*). In fact, this second aphorism is merely a *preliminary* statement intended to kick off the discussion.

The term *citta* is not easily rendered into English. As is the case with so many other Sanskrit terms, there does not seem to be a precise equivalent for it in our vocabulary. Previous translators have proposed a variety of renderings, such as 'mind-stuff', 'thinking-principle' and similar horrific words. In most instances, *citta* seems to convey simply 'consciousness' and perhaps occasionally 'mind'. I have uniformly translated it with the former term. Patañjali, unfortunately, fails to supply us with a definition of this important concept. Still, its meaning can be gathered from the various contexts in which it appears. The following observations can be made:

(1) *Citta* is *not* a genuinely separate category of existence or

[2] By 'soteriology' I mean the body of teachings concerned with liberation.

tattva within the process of cosmic evolution. Alt IV.4 it is said to arise from the 'one mind' (*eka-citta*), has to be identified with the cosmic principle of 'I-am-ne (*asmitā-mātra*), no causal linkage seems to be implied. Rather *citta* is a convenient umbrella concept. This is evident from IV.23.

(2) According to IV.23, *citta* is 'coloured' by the perceived object and the apperceiving Self. In other words, it is in a certain sense created by the transcendental Self-awareness and the insentient objects of the world.

(3) There is not only one *citta*, but a multitude of *cittas* all of which are real (see IV.16) and not merely attributes of the external objects (see IV.15), or products of the projections of a 'single mind' (as in the idealist schools of Buddhism).

(4) *Citta* is 'suffused' with countless 'subliminal-activators' which combine into 'traits' (*vāsanā*) (see IV.24) and which are responsible for the occurrence of the 'fluctuations' (*vṛtti*).

(5) Despite the existence of these 'traits' which force consciousness to externalise itself, it nevertheless serves the purpose of Self-realisation (see IV.24).

(6) When Self-realisation is achieved, the 'primary-constituents' (*guṇa*) 'flow back' into the transcendental world-ground (see IV.34) which implies the destruction not only of the individual organism but also of the consciousness of the liberated being.

As will be appreciated, Patañjali's concept of consciousness is highly sophisticated, though not unproblematic. But, then, the nature of consciousness is one of the great mysteries of human existence. At any rate, for the practical purpose of yogic interiorisation, Patañjali's dynamic model of consciousness is perfectly adequate.

Like *citta*, the term *vṛtti* is not used loosely in the *Yoga-Sūtra*. On the contrary, it is a technical term. It does not refer to any mental activity whatsoever, but only to the five kinds of 'fluctuations' listed in I.6. Patañjali also uses this word in a more general sense (see II.15; 50 and III. 43)—a distinction which has often been glossed over.

Finally, *nirodha* or 'restriction' is similarly a technical term. Much misunderstanding and confusion could have been avoided if it had been realised that *nirodha* stands for both the *process* of restriction and the *state* of restrictedness. In the present aphorism it is definitely

nse, and for this reason it cannot possibly be
ion of the ultimate goal of Yoga. *Nirodha*, in
ls of application:

—restriction of the 'fluctuations'
dha—restriction of the 'presented-ideas'
rodha—restriction of the 'subliminal-activators'
a—complete restriction, coinciding with Self-

The first degree of restriction is achieved by 'meditative-absorption' (*dhyāna*) (see II.11); the second by the lower form of object-oriented enstasy (*saṃprajñāta-samādhi*); the third by the higher type of subject-oriented enstasy (*asaṃprajñāta-samādhi*) and the last by the transition into the culminating 'cloud of *dharma* enstasy' which is immediately followed by Self-realisation.

I.3 *tadā draṣṭuḥ sva-rūpe'vasthānam*

tadā = then
draṣṭṛ = seer (from √*dṛś* 'to see')
sva = own } essence
rūpa = form }
avasthāna = appearing, abiding (from *ava* + √*sthā* 'to stand')

Then the seer [i.e. the Self] abides in [its] essence.

In view of the fact that the preceding aphorism does not speak of the restriction of *all* consciousness activity, the word 'then' (*tadā*) cannot possibly be thought to refer to the condition of *vṛtti-nirodha*. For the Self does not reveal itself in its pure essence as sheer Awareness until *all* conscious activity (not only the fluctuations) has been thoroughly suspended. Admittedly, there is a certain unexpected hiatus between I.2 and I.3, but this kind of logical jump can be excused on the grounds that it is in the nature of an aphoristic work to be as concise as possible.

I.4 *vṛtti-sārūpyam-itaratra*

vṛtti = fluctuation (see I.2)
sārūpya = conformity (from *sa* + *rūpa* 'form')
itaratra = otherwise, here: at other times (locative of *itara*)

At other times [there is] conformity [of the Self] with the fluctuations [of consciousness].

'At other times' simply refers to the particular mode of consciousness in which 'fluctuations' are present. 'Conformity' is not straightforward 'identity'. The Self (*puruṣa*) is by definition always itself and incapable of change. However, to the finite mind it appears as if the Self can be lost or gained, lose itself or realise itself. Yet, if Self-awareness is on no account ever forfeited, how is it to be explained that we in fact experience ourselves as conscious organisms in space and time and not as pure, transcendental Selves? Patañjali does not pretend to have an explanation of this fundamental enigma. In the spirit of a true existential philosopher, he merely observes that we are born ignorant of our essential being, the Self, and that this nescience (*avidyā*) is the root of all our anxiety and suffering. This clouding over of the Self is what is meant by the term *sārūpya*. The loss of Self-awareness is apparent, not actual. A popular simile to explain this strange truth is that of a lake which, on a windless day, reflects the sun without distortion; however, as soon as gusts break up the calm surface of the lake into irregular wave patterns, the sun's reflected image becomes distorted.

I.5 *vṛttayaḥ pañcatayaḥ kliṣṭa-akliṣṭāḥ*

vṛtti = fluctuation (see I.2)
pañca-taya = fivefold (from *pañca* 'five')
kliṣṭa = afflicted (from √*kliś* 'to trouble/be troubled')
akliṣṭa = non-afflicted (from *a* + √*kliś*)

The fluctuations are fivefold; afflicted or non-afflicted.

The five types of 'fluctuation', named in the next aphorism, can be regarded from yet another, more comprehensive viewpoint. They pertain to either of two categories insofar as they may be 'afflicted' or 'non-afflicted'. This word pair has been translated quite differently in the past. Some translators understand it as 'painful/not painful', others as 'distressing/not distressing', etc. For a deeper understanding we need to connect *kliṣṭa*/*akliṣṭa* with the concept of *kleśa* which is of cardinal importance in Patañjali's Kriyā-Yoga. He distinguishes (see II.3) five kinds of *kleśas* or 'causes-of-affliction'. These are the basic motivational forces which prompt a person to act, think, feel. The chief commentator of the *Yoga-Sūtra*, Vyāsa, explains *kliṣṭa* as 'caused by the causes-of-affliction' (*kleśa-hetuka*), but this is unconvincing. For we would have to assume that *akliṣṭa* consequently means 'not caused by the causes-of-affliction'. Yet we know already that the *kleśas* underly all human activity, however spiritual, and therefore are necessarily also responsible for the production of the fluctuations of consciousness. A more congenial answer is given by a later commentator, Rāmānanda, who in his *Maṇiprabhā* defines *kliṣṭa* as 'resulting in bondage' (*bandha-phala*). *Akliṣṭa*, on the other hand, is said by him to refer to that mental activity which facilitates the yogic process of interiorisation and Self-realisation. This presupposes that the causes-of-affliction contain the possibility of self-destruction; otherwise liberation could never be possible. This is in fact admitted by Patañjali (see IV.24) when he concedes that consciousness serves the purpose of Self-realisation.

Presumably all five types of fluctuations can be either 'afflicted' or 'non-afflicted'. For, theoretically at least, one can imagine a situation in which a particular 'misconception' could indirectly prove helpful to the practice of Yoga and thus belong to the *akliṣṭa* category. Even 'sleep' could be attributed with such a positive function, as when, for example, a particular dream image acts as a trigger for meditation (see I.38). Unfortunately, the classical commentators and naturally also the host of translators remain silent on this interesting point.

For simplicity's sake I have translated *kliṣṭa/akliṣṭa* with 'afflicted/non-afflicted', although this literal rendering only very inadequately reflects the profound meaning of these two terms.

I.6 *pramāṇa-viparyaya-vikalpa-nidrā-smṛtayaḥ*

pramāṇa = valid-cognition (from *pra* + √*mā* 'to measure')
viparyaya = misconception (from *vi* + *pari* + √*i* 'to go')
vikalpa = conceptualisation (from *vi* + √*kḷp* 'to be fit/serve')
nidrā = sleep (from *ni* + √*drā* 'to sleep')
smṛti = memory (from √*smṛ* 'to remember')

[The five types of fluctuations are:] valid-cognition, misconception, conceptualisation, sleep and memory.

Perpetual movement (*vṛtti*) and transformation (*pariṇāma*) constitute the quintessence of Nature (*prakṛti*). Consciousness activity is a special instance of this overall flux. The *yogin* cannot control this incessant motility of Nature, but he can acquire mastery over, and learn to arrest all movement pertaining to, that small section of Nature which is his psycho-physical organism. Whereas in the post-classical tradition of Haṭhayoga this stoppage of the dynamism of the natural forces of one's personal microcosm is achieved primarily by means of bodily manipulations, Patañjali's approach is through the medium of consciousness—though of course not entirely, as we shall see. (After all, body and mind form an inseparable unity.) His five categories of 'fluctuations' must be viewed from this practical angle. They are not intended as an exhaustive catalogue of the modes and functions of consciousness.

I.7 *pratyakṣa-anumāna-āgamāḥ pramāṇāni*
pratyakṣa = perception (from *prati* + *akṣa* 'eye')
anumāna = inference (from *anu* + √*mā* 'to measure')
āgama = lit. 'coming up', tradition, here: testimony (from *ā* + √*gam* 'to go')
pramāṇa = valid-cognition (see I.6)
Valid-cognition [is based on] perception, inference and testimony.

How do we know? This question must sooner or later be tackled by any thinker who intends to be taken seriously. It is significant that none of the great philosophical traditions of India has failed to consider the problem of epistemology and to provide its own answer to the question about the possibility of knowledge. This *sūtra* states Patañjali's particular viewpoint about the sources of valid knowledge, and this shows that he was fully aware of the importance of this critical theoretical issue. That he does not go into any detail is understandable, considering the different emphasis of his work.

To make sense of this aphorism, we must take *pramāṇa* to mean 'valid cognition', although it usually stands for the *sources* of correct knowledge. Traditionally, the cognitive process is broken up into five components, viz.

(1) *pramātṛ*—the cognising subject
(2) *prameya*—the cognised object
(3) *pramāṇa*—the instrument of cognition
(4) *pramā*—cognition
(5) *pramānya*—the validity of the cognition

Different sources of valid cognition are admitted in the various schools of thought. The Materialists permit only perception and reject all other means, even inference, as inadequate tools for obtaining correct knowledge. By contrast, in Vedānta six sources of valid cognition are recognised, viz. perception (*pratyakṣa*), inference (*anumāna*), testimony (*śabda*), analogy (*upamāna*), implication (*arthāpatti*) and non-apprehension (*anupalabdhi*).[3] However, both Yoga and Sāṃkhya acknowledge only the first three of this series.

[3] For a detailed discussion of these concepts see Swāmī Satprakāshānanda (1965), pp. 153ff.

I.8. *viparyayo mithyā-jñānam-atad-rūpa-pratiṣṭham*

viparyaya = misconception (see I.6)
mithyā = false, erroneous (from √*mith* 'to conflict with')
jñāna = knowledge (from √*jña* 'to know')
a-tad = not that
rūpa = form, appearance
pratiṣṭha = steadfast, here: based on (from *pra* + √*sthā* 'to stand')

Misconception is erroneous knowledge not based on the [actual] appearance of that [which is the underlying object].

Although this aphorism is discussed at great length by Vācaspati Miśra, its meaning is sufficiently clear not to require any explanation.

I.9 *śabda-jñāna-anupātī vastu-śūnyo vikalpaḥ*

śabda = lit. 'sound', here: verbal
jñāna = knowledge (see I.8)
anupātin = following (from *anu* + √*pat* 'to fall')
vastu = object (from √*vas* 'to remain')
śūnya = void, here: without (from √*śvi* 'to swell')
vikalpa = conceptualisation (see I.6)

Conceptualisation is without [perceivable] object, following [entirely] verbal knowledge.

Conceptualisation ranges from day-dreaming to abstract thinking. Even when the senses do not supply us with information, the formation of thoughts and ideas continues nevertheless. *Vikalpa* definitely means more than 'fancy' (I. K. Taimni) or 'hallucination' (R. S. Mishra). It is our incessant conceptualising of reality in terms of language, which is the most powerful obstacle preventing us from experiencing reality as it really is. However, *vikalpa* is by no means unconditionally worthless. For unless we have a concept of a 'higher Self' or a 'path', we cannot exercise our will to overcome the limitations of conceptual thinking and to break through to the level of the transcendental Self. Clearly, conceptualisation can be either *kliṣṭa* or *akliṣṭa*.

I.10 *abhāva-pratyaya-ālambanā vṛttir-nidrā*

abhāva = lit. 'not-becoming', here: non-occurrence (from *a* + √*bhū* 'to be')
pratyaya = notion, presented-idea (from *prati* + √*i* 'to go')

ālambana = foundation, here: founded on (from *ā* + √*lamb* 'to rest on')
vṛtti = fluctuation (see I.2)
nidrā = sleep (see I.6)

Sleep is a fluctuation founded on the presented-idea of the non-occurrence [of other contents of consciousness].

Contrary to I. K. Taimni's (1961) opinion, the meaning of this aphorism is not readily apparent. The difficulty lies in the phrase *abhāva-pratyaya* which most translators have taken to mean 'absence of presented-ideas'. But already Vyāsa observes that one must assume some kind of experience of a presented-idea in sleep, or how else could one recollect that one has slept well or badly as the case may be? Nor will it do to interpret the word *pratyaya* as 'cause'. In sleep, a particular type of presented-idea is said to be present, namely the presented-idea of 'non-becoming', that is to say, of the non-occurrence of any other consciousness activity. Without this assumption of a rudimentary sort of awareness in sleep, it would be difficult to distinguish sleep from the state of *nirodha*.

I.11 *anubhūta-viṣaya-asaṃpramoṣaḥ smṛtiḥ*
anubhūta = experienced (from *anu* + √*bhū* 'to be')
viṣaya = object (from √*viṣ* 'to be active' + *aya* 'going')
asaṃpramoṣa = non-stealing (from *a* + *sam* + *pra* + √*muṣ* 'to steal'), here: non-deprivation
smṛti = memory, here: remembering (see I.6)

Remembering is the non-deprivation of the experienced object.

This aphorism defines the last of the five types of 'fluctuations' with the help of a vivid image taken from everyday experience. When we try to remember a particular item we occasionally find that just as it is about to appear, as a memory icon, on the horizon of our consciousness, it is being snatched back as it were by an irresistible force. This is the well-known 'tip of the tongue' phenomenon. Patañjali looks upon this process as a kind of 'theft' (*pramoṣa*). Remembering, on the other hand, is the successful retrieval of forgotten events or things. It is preferable to translate *smṛti* in the present context with 'remembering' rather than 'memory'. The latter term is best reserved for the network of subconscious traits (*vāsanā*) which make recollection possible. According to Vyāsa the presented-ideas (*pratyaya*), which are the units of all conscious experiencing (including sleep), give rise to corresponding subliminal-activators (*saṃskāra*). Their totality constitutes what I wish to call the depth-memory (*smṛti*), or the subconscious, as spoken of in aphorism I.43.

I.12 *abhyāsa-vairāgyābhyāṃ tan-nirodhaḥ*

abhyāsa = practice (from *abhi* + √*ās* 'to apply oneself')
vairāgya = dispassion (from *vai* 'dis-' + √*raj* 'be attracted, excited' + *ya*)
tad = that, here: these
nirodha = restriction (see I.2)

The restriction of these [fluctuations] [is achieved] through practice and dispassion.

Practice and dispassion stand for the two poles of any form of yogic discipline. The former represents the endeavour to actualise the Self by means of techniques of interiorisation and unification; the latter represents the corresponding attitude of letting go of the hunger for the external world of multiplicity. As I have observed elsewhere,[4]

Practice without dispassion is conducive to an abnormal ego-inflation and hunger for power and thus increased entanglement in things worldly. Dispassion without practice, on the other hand, is like a blunt knife; the psychosomatic energies generated through the turning away from mundane objects remain without an outlet and at best cause confusion in body and mind. Both poles need to be cultivated simultaneously and with prudence.

I.13 *tatra sthitau yatno'bhyāsaḥ*

tatra = in that (from *ta*)
sthiti = stability (from √*sthā* 'to stand')
yatna = exertion, effort (from √*yat* 'to marshal')
abhyāsa = practice (see I.12)

Practice is the exertion [in gaining] stability in that [state of restriction].

Practice is an effort of will to reach and abide in the condition of 'restriction' (*nirodha*), not merely the restriction of the fluctuations but, ultimately, of all mental activity. The supreme goal is the stopping of the vibrations of the microcosm as such.

I.14 *sa tu dīrgha-kāla-nairantarya-satkāra-āsevito dṛḍha-bhūmiḥ*

sa = it, here: this (from *tad*)
tu = but

[4] See G. Feuerstein (1974[a]), p. 36.

dīrgha = long
kāla = time (from √*kal* 'to impel')
nairantarya = continuance, here: uninterruptedly (from *nair* + *antar* 'between' + *ya*, lit. 'non-between-ness')
sat-kāra = right fashion, here: properly (from *sat* 'right' + √*kṛ* 'to do')
āsevita = cultivated (from *ā* + √*sev* 'to resort to')
dṛḍha = firm, firmly (from √*dṛṃh* 'to fasten')
bhūmi = earth, here: grounded (from √*bhū* 'to become')

But this [practice] is firmly grounded [only after it has been] cultivated properly and for a long time uninterruptedly.

Practice does not mean occasional exercising. It is persevering application, a long-term dedication. The natural tendency of our consciousness is to flow outwards, and the central objective of practice or *abhyāsa* is to reverse this propensity by establishing a counter-habit of inward-mindedness or *pratyakcetanā* (see I.29). This alone makes Self-realisation possible. For, as is continually reiterated by the scriptures of Yoga, the Self is not to be found in the outside world. Rather it is the nucleus of our inmost being and hence cannot possibly be a sensory datum. Meister Eckehart, one of the great mystics of the Christian tradition, speaks of the 'spark' buried deep within the soul never touched by space or time.

I.15 *dṛṣṭa-ānuśravika-viṣaya-vitṛṣṇasya vaśīkāra-saṃjñā vairāgyam*

dṛṣṭa = seen (from √*dṛś* 'to see')
ānuśravika = revealed (from *anu* + √*śru* 'to hear, learn')
viṣaya = object (see I.11)
vitṛṣṇa = the thirstless, here: without thirst (from *vi* + √*tṛṣ* 'to be thirsty')
vaśīkāra = mastery (from √*vaś* 'to will' + √*kṛ* 'to make', lit. 'making-willing')
saṃjñā = knowledge (from *sam* + √*jña* 'to know')
vairāgya = dispassion (see I.12)

Dispassion is the knowledge-of-mastery of [that *yogin* who is] without thirst for seen [*i.e.* earthly] and revealed objects.

Patañjali specifies here the two types of objects in regard to which the *yogin* must develop perfect dispassion, namely the 'seen' objects of the external world and the 'revealed' things promised in the sacred texts. The yogic non-attachment extends to the objects and pleasures of the heavenly regions, since the *yogin* does not aspire to any of the numerous angelic estates known to traditional religion but seeks to transcend both the realm of man and the realm of angels (*deva*) in order to win through to what the Buddha called 'the sphere where there is neither earth nor water nor fire nor air; neither the sphere of space-infinity nor the sphere of consciousness-infinity nor the sphere of nothingness . . .'[5] As is evident from the phrase 'knowledge of mastery', dispassion means more than occasional dislike or intermittent withdrawal; it represents a genuine achievement securely anchored in the depths of one's being—not simply world flight but world transcendence; not neurotic self-encapsulation but the conscious re-alignment of one's entire life in the light of higher values; the quenching of the craving for ephemeral things.

I.16 *tat-paraṃ puruṣa-khyāter-guṇa-vaitṛṣṇyam*

tad = that, here: this
para = superior
puruṣa = Self (lit. 'man', etymology unknown)
khyāti = vision (from √*khyā* 'to be known')
guṇa = primary-constituent (lit. 'strand')
vaitṛṣṇya = non-thirsting (a synonym of *vitṛṣṇa*, see I.15)

The superior [form] of this [dispassion] is the non-thirsting for the primary-constituents [of Nature] [which results] from the vision of the Self.

Stanza II.59 from the *Bhagavad-Gītā*, the most popular of all Yoga texts, explains what is meant here: 'For the body-essence (*dehin*) who ceases to "eat", the objects disappear, except for the relish (*rasa*). The relish also disappears for him when the Supreme is beheld.'

Ordinary or partial dispassion does not destroy the subliminal-activators (*saṃskāra*) and therefore cannot be considered as absolutely secured. However, with the higher form of dispassion, which coincides with the state of *asaṃprajñāta-samādhi* (see IV.29), the possibility of renewed attachment to worldly and heavenly things is eliminated. This is effected by the *yogin*'s profound identity shift from the ego or self of the psychosomatic organism to the transcendental Self. *Para-vairāgya* is thus a decided No to the world (*prakṛti*) as such. Not everybody is able to make this radical negation (see I.19). 'Vision of the Self' means the same as 'Self-realisation', that

[5] *Udāna* VIII.1 (Pāli Text Society edition, p. 80).

is, the establishment of pure awareness (*cit*) in consciousness (*citta*). This is not a particularly happy way of conceptualising these elusive processes in the higher states of enstasy, but Patañjali's strictly dualistic metaphysics leaves us little option. However, I am convinced that the phenomenological study of altered states of consciousness will, before long, furnish a more adequate model. Besides, even in avowedly non-dualistic systems of thought such as Advaita-Vedānta we can find numerous examples of basically dualistic modes of description and explanation.

The nature of the primary-constituents (*guṇa*), which are the ultimate, irreducible building blocks of the material and mental world, has been explained in the Introduction (see pp. 15f).

I.17 *vitarka-vicāra-ānanda-asmitā-(rūpa-) anugamāt-saṃprajñātaḥ*

vitarka = cogitation (from *vi* + √*tark* 'to reflect')
vicāra = reflection (from *vi* + √*car* 'to move')
ānanda = joy (from *ā* + √*nand* 'to be happy')
asmitā = lit. 'I-am-ness' (from *asmi* 'I am' + *tā* 'ness')
[*rūpa* = form (this word is absent in many editions)]
anugama = connected (from *anu* + √*gam* 'to go')
saṃprajñāta = cognitive (from *sam* + *prajñā* 'knowledge, gnosis')

[The enstasy arising out of the state of restriction] is cognitive [i.e. object-oriented] by being connected with [the forms of] cogitation, reflection, joy or I-am-ness.

What happens when the five types of 'fluctuations' are fully suspended, when, in other words, consciousness has fallen back on itself? Yoga adamantly denies that *nirodha* results in, or is equivalent to, mere catalepsy or trance, etc. Rather it is conceived as a state of 'readiness' in which consciousness opens itself to the possibility of a new mode of experience, known as enstasy or *samādhi*. However, *nirodha* is only a *necessary*, not a *sufficient* precondition for the enstatic consciousness. It appears that the 'grace' of the 'lord' (*īśvara*) is also required (see II.45).

Not every enstasy reveals the Self. Basically, *samādhi* represents an alternative mode of experiencing to our day-to-day consciousness in which subject and object are always distinct. This fundamental dichotomy is overcome in enstasy, and the object is experienced from within, as it were. The characteristic feature of enstasy is thus the experiential identification of subject and object (see I.41). This is not a nebulous process but one accompanied by supra-wakefulness. In fact it is this acute awareness and feeling of reality which typifies the enstatic experience and differentiates it from other ordinary and non-ordinary forms of consciousness.

Patañjali distinguishes two basic types of enstasy, *viz. saṃprajñāta-samādhi* or cognitive enstasy and *asaṃprajñāta-samādhi* or ultra-cognitive enstasy. The former has an objective mainstay or 'prop' which may be any of the myriads of forms of Nature, including the transcendental core of the world itself. The latter type of enstasy, on the other hand, has no objective support whatsoever but is entirely oriented towards the Self. According to the *Yoga-Sūtra* the conscious activity in the enstatic mode of experience can take four forms, viz. cogitation, reflection, joy or I-am-ness. These are of course not 'fluctuations' (*vṛtti*) in the sense defined above. Rather they belong to the category of *prajñā* or 'supra-cognition, gnosis'.

Vitarka or 'cogitation' refers to that supra-cognition which occurs in enstasy when the object pertains to the visible realm of Nature. *Vicāra* or 'reflection' applies to those enstatic processes which focus on an object drawn from the deep structure of Nature, such as the 'energy potentials' (*tanmātra*) or the senses (*indriya*). 'Joy' and 'I-am-ness', however, must be regarded as accompanying phenomena of every cognitive enstasy. The explanations of the classical commentators on this point appear to be foreign to Patañjali's hierarchy of enstatic states, and it seems unlikely that *ānanda* and *asmitā* should constitute independent levels of *samādhi*. The practice of cognitive enstasy prepares the *yogin* for the higher form of *samādhi* which is referred to in the next aphorism.

I.18 *virāma-pratyaya-abhyāsa-pūrvaḥ saṃskāra-śeṣo'nyaḥ*

virāma = cessation (from *vi* + √*ram* 'to stop')
pratyaya = presented-idea (see I.10)
abhyāsa = practice (see I.12)
pūrva = former
saṃskāra = subliminal-activator (from *sam* = √*kṛ* 'to do')
śeṣa = residuum (from √*śiṣ* 'to remain')
anya = other

The other [type of enstasy] has a residuum of subliminal-activators; [it follows] the former [cognitive enstasy] upon the practice of the presented-idea of cessation.

The 'other' type of enstasy is *asaṃprajñāta-samādhi* in which consciousness is devoid of all objective supports and exists merely in the form of the subliminal-activators. This elevated state is said to ensue from the 'practice of the presented-idea of cessation', which sounds more obscure than it is. The compound *virāma-pratyaya-abhyāsa* has been misinterpreted by the classical commentators who take *pratyaya* to mean 'cause' and also confuse 'cessation' with 'restriction' (*nirodha*). Clearly, *asaṃprajñāta* follows upon *saṃprajñāta-samādhi* and not upon the restriction of the fluctuations which is achieved in meditative absorption.

But what is a 'presented-idea of cessation'? Just as in sleep there is a presented-idea of 'non-occurrence' (see I.10), so also in the higher stages of cognitive enstasy there is an awareness of the gradual inhibition of all presented-ideas. Upon full restriction of all presented-ideas, cognitive enstasy converts into ultra-cognitive enstasy.

It is misleading to render *asaṃprajñāta-samādhi* by 'unconscious', as M. N. Dvivedī and other earlier translators have done. Although this superior mode of enstatic consciousness implies the demolition of the ordinary consciousness of objects (or consciousness-of), there is nonetheless consciousness in the shape of the root-consciousness (*cit*) or Self-awareness. The term *asaṃprajñāta* is meant to convey the transcendence of all forms of supra-cognition (*prajñā*). What is left of consciousness (*citta*) in this state is its deep structure, that is, the network of subliminal-activators (*saṃskāra*). Their restriction and ultimate annihilation is achieved by the prolonged practice of ultra-cognitive enstasy (see I.50–1). At this point the identity of the *yogin* has almost completely shifted to the Self, and there seems to be merely a marginal awareness of the mind complex or what is left of it in this culminatory experience.

I.19 *bhava-pratyayo videha-prakṛti-layānām*

bhava = becoming (from √*bhū* 'to be')
pratyaya = presented-idea (see I.10)
videha = bodiless (from *vi* + √*dih* 'to cover, smear'; *deha* = body)
prakṛti = nature, here: world-ground (from *pra* + √*kṛ* 'to make, perform'; lit. 'procreativity')
laya = dissolved, merged (from √*lī* 'to clasp, be absorbed')

[The enstasy of those who have] merged with the world-ground [and those who are] bodiless [is due to the persistence of] the presented-idea of becoming.

The *sūtra* refers to those *yogins* who have become side-tracked and, instead of reaching the Self, have found a false identity in one or other manifestation of Nature. Those who identify with the transcendental core of the world are known as *prakṛti-laya*; all others are called *videha* or 'bodiless'. One may conjecture that this includes the many angelic beings (*deva*) whose tempting invitations the *yogin* is being warned against by Patañjali (see III.51). Their failure to achieve emancipation is due to the presence of presented-ideas of 'becoming' in their minds instead of presented-ideas of 'cessation'. J. H. Woods wrongly assumes this enstasy to be of the ultra-cognitive type.

I.20 *śraddhā-vīrya-smṛti-samādhi-prajñā-pūrvaka itareṣām*

śraddhā = faith (from √*śrat* 'to assure' + √*dhā* 'to put')
vīrya = energy (from √*vī* 'to approach eagerly' + *ya*)
smṛti = memory, here: mindfulness (see I.6)
samādhi =(cognitive) enstasy (from *sam* + *ā* + √*dhā* 'to put'; lit. 'putting together')
prajñā = supra-cognition (from *pra* + √*jña* 'to know')
pūrvaka = preceding, here: preceded by
itara = other

[The enstasy] of the others [*i.e.* those *yogins* whose path is described in I.18] is preceded by faith, energy, mindfulness, enstasy and supra-cognition.

In contrast to the *yogins* mentioned in I.19 who have entered a state of quasi-liberation, those who succeed in reaching genuine Self-awareness ground their practice on the cultivation of the following five features of the path:

(1) Faith or a positive attitude towards the yogic way of life which, as Vyāsa observes, protects the *yogin* like a caring mother;
(2) energy or the vitality arising from faith;
(3) mindfulness or the practice of concentration and meditation;
(4) enstasy, by which is meant cognitive enstasy or *saṃprajñāta-samādhi*;
(5) supra-cognition or gnosis, that is, the kind of enstatic knowledge which is conducive to Self-realisation.

These five factors are also known to the buddhist tradition, and it has been suggested that Patañjali adopted them from there. However, it seems equally likely that this set, like so many other notions, is not particular to any one tradition. It must be added that the above interpretation differs from the buddhist explanation of this pentad.

I.21 *tīvra-saṃvegānām-āsannaḥ*

tīvra = extreme, here: extremely
saṃvega = vehemence, here: vehement (from *sam* + √*vij* 'to be agitated')
āsanna = near (*ā* + √*sad* 'to sit')

[This supreme enstasy] is near to [him who is] extremely vehement [in his practice of Yoga].

The *yogin*'s success depends on the intensity of his commitment to the cultivation of *abhyāsa* and *vairāgya* or the practice of unification and dispassion towards the manifold things of the world. The term *saṃvega* is explained by the Jaina author Hemacandra in his *Yoga-Śāstra* (II.15) as 'the desire for emancipation' (*mokṣa-abhilāsa*). This interpretation makes sense also within the context of Classical Yoga and should be considered as a suitable alternative to the above translation. At any rate, the 'vehemence' spoken of in this aphorism has nothing to do with excessive asceticism or pathological mortification. It is enthusiasm in the best sense of the word.

I.22 *mṛdu-madhya-adhimātratvāt-tato'pi viśeṣaḥ*

mṛdu = modest (from √*mṛd* 'to crush')
madhya = medium
adhimātratva = excessiveness, here: excessive (from *adhi* + *mātra* 'measure')
tatas = hence (from *ta* which is the pronoun of the third person)
api = also
viśeṣa = difference (from *vi* + √*śiṣ* 'to remain')

Because [this vehemence can be] modest, medium or excessive, [there is] hence also a difference [in the proximity of the ***yogins*** **to the superior enstasy].**

Contrary to the opinion of J. H. Woods, who follows the cues of the commentaries, this aphorism does not refer to a special kind of enstasy, but merely develops the idea of the previous *sūtra*. It is simply intended to drive home the importance of *saṃvega* and should not be deemed as a platitudinous and unnecessary adjunct.

I.23 *īśvara-praṇidhānād-vā*

īśvara = lord (from √*īś* 'to own, be master of' + *vara* 'choicest' from √*vṛ* 'to choose')
praṇidhāna = resolution, here: devotion (from *pra* + *ni* + √*dhā* 'to put')
vā = or

Or [enstasy is gained] through devotion to the Lord.

Although all schools of hindu Yoga recognise the existence of a supreme being, variously referred to as *īś, īśa, īśana* or *īśvara*, this belief does not in every case find expression in the actual discipline of Yoga. Whether or not the Lord is regarded as an archetypal model to be emulated in the form of active devotion (*praṇidhāna*) appears to be a question of personal choice. Hence the word 'or' to initiate the present aphorism. J. W. Hauer is mistaken in taking the practice of devotion to the Lord as an alternative discipline to *abhyāsa* and *vairāgya* (see I.12). It is at best an alternative to the five factors mentioned in I.20. Probably, however, the word *vā* has to be understood in the sense of 'or more specifically', which makes *īśvara-praṇidhāna* a particular instance of the category of *abhyāsa*.

What this devotion consists in is not absolutely clear. It may signify a general attitude of respectful emulation of the archetypal *yogin* or perhaps a loving imitation (*bhakti*) finding concrete expression in acts of worship in which the *īśvara* fulfils the function of the deity of popular religion.

I.24 *kleśa-karma-vipāka-āsayair-aparāmṛṣṭaḥ puruṣa-viśeṣa īśvaraḥ*

kleśa = cause-of-affliction (from √*kliś* 'to trouble/be troubled')
karman = action (from √*kṛ* 'to do')
vipāka = fruition (from *vi* + √*pac* 'to cook, ripen')
āśaya = resting-place, here: deposit (from *ā* + √*śī* 'to lie, rest')
aparāmṛṣṭa = untouched (from *a* + *parā* + √*mṛś* 'to touch')
puruṣa = Self (see I.16)
viśeṣa = special (see I.22)
īśvara = lord (see I.23)

The Lord is a special Self [because he is] untouched by the causes-of-affliction, action [and its] fruition [and by] the deposit [in the depth-memory].

Here Patañjali explains the concept of *īśvara.* First of all, far from being a product of insentient Nature (*prakṛti*), the Lord is regarded as a special Self. His uniqueness lies in the fact that he has never been, nor will ever be, touched by the mechanisms of Nature. He has at no time been subject to the causes-of affliction (see II.3–9), to action and its inevitable consequences in terms of the generation of subliminal-activators deposited in the subconscious. In other words, the Lord stands beyond the wheel of existence. In a certain sense this is also true of the *puruṣa,* man's innermost essence. However, unlike any other Self, the Lord has never suffered from the delusion that he is unfree, in bondage to the limiting forms of Nature.

I.25 *tatra niratiśayaṃ sarva-jña-bījam*

tatra = in that, here: in Him (from *ta*)
niratiśaya = unsurpassed (from *nir* + *ati* + √*śī* 'to lie, rest')
sarva = all } here: omniscience
jña = knowing (from √*jña* 'to know') } here: omniscience
bīja = seed

In Him the seed of omniscience is unsurpassed.

With this aphorism Patañjali seeks to ensure the supremacy of the Lord by asserting that he is the upper limit of the potential of omniscience innate in man. This is neither a 'proof' for the existence of God, as often thought, nor a statement to the effect that omniscience is graded, which would be plainly tautological. More probably, this is another way of asserting the archetypal function of *īśvara* whose lofty existence serves the *yogin* as a model and standard.

I.26 *pūrveṣām-api guruḥ kālena-anavacchedāt*

pūrva = former, here: earlier
api = also
guru = mentor (as adjective meaning 'heavy', from √*gur* 'to call on')
kāla = time, here: temporal (from √*kal* 'to impel, urge')
anavaccheda = continuity (from *an* + *ava* + √*chid* 'to cut'; lit. 'non-boundedness')

[The Lord] was also the mentor of the earlier [*yogins*] by virtue of [His] temporal continuity.

How can the Lord be said to be wholly transcendental and yet be regarded as the teacher of the ancient sages? This apparent contradiction can be resolved quite easily by taking his role as instructor in a metaphorical and not a literal sense. His teaching is by way of what M. Eliade called a 'metaphysical sympathy', an incomprehensible attraction which his essence exercises on the *yogin*. This silent communication is possible because of the transcendental co-essentiality of the very being of *īśvara* and the Self. On the empirical level this is expressed in the idealisation of the Lord as arch-*yogin* and ever-present example.

I.27 *tasya vācakaḥ praṇavaḥ*

tasya = his (from *tad*)
vācaka = symbol (from √*vac* 'to speak'; literally 'speaking, denoting')
praṇava = lit. 'pronouncement' (from *pra* + √*nu* 'to shout, exult'), here: left untranslated

His symbol is the *praṇava* [i.e. **the syllable** *oṃ*].

Since the very earliest times the sages of India have symbolised the Absolute by the morpheme *oṃ*, the classic hindu *mantra*, also known in the sacred literature as the *praṇava*. According to esoteric speculation, the sound *oṃ* is a composite of the letters *a* + *u* + *m* to which must be added as a fourth element the peculiar humming of *m* (technically referred to as the *anusvāra*, from √*svar* 'to sound', or nasalisation). The humming of *oṃ* is in fact one of the oldest and most widely practised techniques of Yoga.

I.28 *taj-japas-tad-artha-bhāvanam*

tad = that
japas = recitation (from √*jap* 'to repeat, mutter')
tad = that, here: its
artha = meaning (from √*arth* 'to intend'?)
bhāvana = realisation, here: contemplation (from √*bhū* 'to become')

The recitation of that [syllable] [leads to] the contemplation of its meaning.

The exact meaning of this aphorism cannot be made out. The classical commentators understand it in the following way: 'Repetition of it [and] reflection upon its meaning [should be made].' What seems to be implied in this *sūtra* is the idea that the constant repetition or recitation of the syllable *oṃ* is not enough in itself. It must be performed in a meditative frame of mind in order to become an authentic instrument of internalisation.

I.29 *tataḥ pratyakcetanā-adhigamo'py-antarāya-abhāvaś-ca*

tatas = thence (from *ta*)
pratyak-cetanā = reverse/inward-mindedness (from *prati* + √*ac* 'to bend' + √*cit* 'to be conscious')
adhigama = attainment (from *adhi* + √*gam* 'to go')
api = also
antarāya = obstacle (from *antar* 'between' + √*ī* 'to go', lit. 'get between')
abhāva = disappearance (from *a* + √*bhū* 'to become')
ca = and

Thence [follows] the attainment of [habitual] inward-mindedness and also the disappearance of the obstacles [mentioned below].

With this aphorism Patañjali returns to the topic of 'restriction' or *nirodha* which presupposes the particular frame of mind known as inward-mindedness or 'reversal' (*pratyaktva*) as the *Tejobindu-Upaniṣad* (I.38) has it. The pursuit of Yoga requires all the dedication, energy and will-power a person can muster, for, as the texts repeatedly warn us, numerous pitfalls await those who set out on the way to Self-realisation. Patañjali lists nine such obstacles.

I.30 *vyādhi-styāna-saṃśaya-pramāda-ālasya-avirati-bhrānti-darśana-alabdha-bhūmikatva-anavasthitatvāni citta-vikṣepās-te'ntarāyāḥ*

vyādhi = sickness (from *vi* + *ā* + √*dhā* 'to put')
styāna = languor (from √*styā* 'to grow dense')
saṃśaya = doubt (from *sam* + √*śī* 'to lie, rest')
pramāda = heedlessness (from *pra* + √*mad* 'to be intoxicated')
ālasya = sloth (from *ā* + √*las* 'to shine')
avirati = dissipation (from *a* + *vi* + √*ram* 'to stop, enjoy oneself')
bhrānti = false (from √*bhram* 'to wander about'; lit. 'wandering off', often in the sense of 'error')
darśana = vision (from √*dṛś* 'to see')
alabdha = lit. 'unobtained', here: non-attaining (from *a* + √*labh* 'to obtain')
bhūmikatva = stage (from √*bhū* 'to become' also meaning 'earth' + *mi* + *ka* + *tva*)
anavasthitatva = instability (from *an* + *ava* + √*sthā* 'to stand')

citta = consciousness (from √*cit* 'to be conscious')
vikṣepa = distraction (from *vi* + √*kṣip* 'to throw, cast')
te = they, here: these (from *tad*)
antarāya = obstacle (from *antar* 'between' + √*i* 'to go')

Sickness, languor, doubt, heedlessness, sloth, dissipation, false vision, non-attaining of the stages [of Yoga] and instability [in these stages] are the distractions of consciousness; these are the obstacles.

Anything that prevents the *yogin* from cultivating the attitude of inward-mindedness[6] is considered as an obstacle, be it physical illness or psychic disorders. Some of these hindrances may develop as a result of wrong practice or over-exertion, but occasionally latent (genetic) weaknesses flare up and handicap the *yogin* who has not been guilty of even the slightest mistake in his practice. Hence the emphatic insistence in the old Sanskrit texts that only the healthy and strong should dedicate their lives to Yoga or, at least, that only they can entertain a realistic hope of success. It is not always understood that meditation, as the keystone of any yogic discipline, is a highly potent instrument which, like nuclear power, can be put to constructive or destructive use. It can lead a person out of his neurotic enmeshments and self-delusions or drag him deeper into confusion and anxiety. In no way is meditation a substitute for work on the integration of one's personality. Genuine Yoga calls for both.

I.31 *duḥkha-daurmanasya-aṅgam-ejayatva-śvāsa-praśvāsā vikṣepa-sahabhuvaḥ*

duḥkha = pain (from *dus* 'bad' + *kha* 'axle-hole')
daurmanasya = depression (from *dus* 'bad' + √*man* 'to think' + *as* + *ya*)
aṅga = limb (or body) (from √*aṅg* 'to stir')
ejayatva = tremor (from √*ej* 'to tremble')
śvāsa = wrong-inhalation (from √*śvas* 'to pant')
praśvāsa = wrong-exhalation (from *pra* + √*śvas* 'to pant')
vikṣepa = distraction (see I.30)
sahabhuva = accompanying (from *saha* 'jointly' + √*bhū* 'to become')

Pain, depression, tremor of the limbs, [wrong] inhalation and exhalation are accompanying [symptoms] of the distractions.

[6] It seems that R. S. Mishra (1972) has misunderstood this important concept, for he translates *pratyakcetanā* with 'cosmic consciousness'.

Faulty Yoga practice can do a great deal of harm, especially to the nervous system, and this is one of the principal reasons why all authorities, past and present, emphasise the importance of a qualified teacher. He will not only monitor the progress of his student but also assess approaching pitfalls and, if and when necessary, give him advance warning of any dangers. Equally importantly, he will also be there to reassure the student when he is in doubt about certain unexpected, but quite normal, developments from his practice of meditation or breath-control.

I.32 *tat-pratiṣedha-artham-eka-tattva-abhyāsaḥ*

tad = that, here: these
pratiṣedha = prevention, here: counteract (from *prati* 'counter' + √*sidh* 'to ward off')
artha = purpose, here: in order to (see I.28)
eka = one, here: single
tattva = lit. 'that-ness', here: principle (from *tad* + *tva*)
abhyāsa = practice (see I.12)

In order to counteract these [distractions] [the *yogin* should resort to] the practice [of concentration] on a single principle.

To prevent or, if the *yogin* happens to be afflicted, to eliminate these disabilities, Patañjali recommends assiduous dedication to single-mindedness. Vyāsa and Vācaspati Miśra go into lengthy polemics against the buddhist notion of the discontinuous nature of consciousness, but lamentably fail to tell us anything of practical interest. However, the general import of this aphorism is clear: Yoga offers a wide choice of techniques and 'props' for concentration, and the *yogin* is free to select whichever method he feels is best suited for his needs and abilities (see I.39). Yet, to avoid unnecessary drawbacks he is advised to stick to one particular meditational 'support' rather than to switch from one topic to another, until he is confident that the introduction of variety into his programme will not be counter-productive.

I.33 *maitrī-karuṇā-muditā-upekṣāṇāṃ sukha-duḥkha-puṇya-apuṇya-viṣayāṇāṃ bhāvanātaś-citta-prasādanam*

maitrī = friendliness (from √*mid* 'to adhere' ?)
karuṇā = compassion (from √*kṛ* 'to do')
muditā = gladness (from √*mud* 'to rejoice')
upekṣā = equanimity (from *upa* + √*īkṣ* 'to see')
sukha = joyful (from *su* 'well' + *kha* 'axle-hole')

duḥkha = pain, here: sorrowful (see I.31)
puṇya = merit, here: meritorious (from √*puṇ* 'to do good')
apuṇya = demerit, here: demeritorious (from *a* + √*puṇ*)
viṣaya = object (see I.11)
bhāvanātas = projecting, here: projection (from √*bhū* 'to become')
citta = consciousness (see I.2)
prasādana = pacification (from *pra* + √*sad* 'to sit')

The projection of friendliness, compassion, gladness and equanimity towards objects—[be they] joyful, sorrowful, meritorious or demeritorious—[bring about] the pacification of consciousness.

Patañjali introduces here a method for tranquillising the mind which is a favourite among buddhist monks and laymen. For instance, in the *Majjhima-Nikāya* (I.38) 'friendliness', 'compassion', 'gladness' and 'equanimity' are collectively referred to as the 'stations of *brahma*' (*brahma-vihāra*). In a special meditational exercise these four virtues are radiated into all corners of the universe for the benefit of all living creatures. The term *upekṣā* requires a brief comment. It does not stand for mere 'indifference', as I. K. Taimni and many other translators would have it, but is denotative of a more subtle and positive attitude, namely a dispassionate but nonetheless empathetic witnessing of mundane events.

I.34 *pracchardana-vidhāraṇābhyāṃ vā prāṇasya*

pracchardana = expulsion (from *pra* + √*chrid* 'to vomit, expel')
vidhāraṇa = retention (from *vi* + √*dhā* 'to put, hold')
vā = or
prāṇa = breath/life-force (from *pra* + √*an* 'to breathe')

Or [restriction is achieved] by [the controlled] expulsion and retention of the breath.

The extraordinary effect of breathing on consciousness has been discovered early on in the history of Yoga, and the speculations about the nature of *prāṇa* date back to the vedic age, that is, more than three millennia ago. *Prāṇa* signifies 'breath' in the pre-modern sense of 'vital-force' rather than the 'oxygen' of contemporary chemistry. Controlled, rhythmic breathing acquired unparalleled importance in Haṭhayoga where it is often combined with special visualisation exercises. (See also *Yoga-Sūtra* II.49–51.)

I.35 *viṣaya-vatī vā pravṛttir-utpannā manasaḥ sthiti-nibandhanī*

viṣaya = object (see I.11)
vatī = feminine form of suffix 'having' (*vant*)
} here: object-centred
vā = or
pravṛtti = activity (from *pra* + √*vṛt* 'to turn')
utpanna = arisen (from *ud* 'up' + √*pad* 'to fall')
manas = mind (from √*man* 'to think')
sthiti = steadiness (from √*sthā* 'to stand')
nibandhanin = holding, here: holds (from *ni* + √*bandh* 'to bind')

Or [restriction comes about when] an object-centred activity has arisen which holds the mind in steadiness.

The classical commentators explain this 'object-centred' activity as a kind of 'supernal perception' (*divya-saṃvid*), or heightened sensory awareness. For example, concentration on the tip of the nose is said to intensify the sense of smell. Boris Sacharow, a German Yoga teacher who practised this method extensively, was apparently able to detect and correctly identify the scent of flowers placed in an adjoining room.[7] Concentration on other sensory organs is held to produce similar experiences with regard to taste, touch, sound, etc. In addition to focusing the mind, this technique, as Vyāsa observes, also helps to dispel any doubts which the novice may harbour regarding the effectiveness of Yoga.

I.36 *viśokā vā jyotiṣmatī*

viśoka = sorrowless (from *vi* + √*śuc* 'to burn')
vā = or
jyotiṣ-matī = illuminating (from √*jyut* 'to shine' + fem. form of suffix *mant* 'having, consisting of'; *jyotis* 'light')

Or [restriction is achieved by mental activities which are] sorrowless and illuminating.

According to Vyāsa this 'activity' follows upon the concentration on the 'lotus of the heart' (*hṛdaya-puṇḍarika*), the 'heart centre' or *hṛd-cakra* in which various light phenomena can be experienced in the state of meditation.

I.37 *vīta-rāga-viṣayaṃ vā cittam*

vīta = without, here: conquered

[7] See B. Sacharow (1957), p. 116.

rāga = attachment (from √*raj* 'to be excited')
viṣaya = object, here: has as its object, is directed to (see I.11)
vā = or
citta = consciousness (see I.2)

Or [restriction is achieved when] consciousness is directed to [those beings who] have conquered attachment.

The compound *vīta-rāga* is traditionally understood to refer to those accomplished *yogins* who, like the sage Nārada, have dropped all passionate attachment and thus are worthy of emulation and make ideal objects of yogic concentration. However, this phrase could also denote '[things] which do not incite passion or attachment', as J. W. Hauer (1958) points out.

I.38 *svapna-nidrā-jñāna-ālambanaṃ vā*

svapna = dream (from √*svap* 'to sleep')
nidrā = sleep (from *ni* + √*drā* 'to sleep')
jñāna = knowledge, here: insight (see I.8)
ālambana = holding, here: resting on (from *ā* + √*lamb* 'to hang')
vā = or

Or [restriction is achieved when consciousness] is resting on the insight [arising from] dreams and sleep.

Rather like psychoanalysis or psychotherapy, the practice of Yoga involves the whole person, not only his waking consciousness but also the subconscious. The yogin's spiritual quest entails a complete reorientation of his entire life which, unsurprisingly, is also reflected in his dreams which become more vivid and charged with meaning. Moreover, his sleep acquires a remarkable lucidity and becomes the stepping-stone for spontaneous meditative experiences.

I.39 *yathā-abhimata-dhyānād-vā*

yathā = as
abhimata = desired (from *abhi* + √*man* 'to think')
dhyāna = meditation, here: meditative-absorption (from √*dhyai* 'to meditate')
vā = or

Or [restriction is achieved] through meditative-absorption as desired.

Patañjali has mentioned a number of well-tried ways of achieving the state of restriction (*nirodha*). In this aphorism he declares that any object whatsoever can serve as a prop for concentration as long as it is found to be of practical expediency.

I.40 *parama-aṇu-parama-mahatva-anto'sya vaśīkāraḥ*

parama = extreme, here: most (from √*pṛ* 'to surpass')
aṇu = minute
parama = here: greatest (see above)
mahatva = lit. greatness, here: magnitude (from √*mah* 'to magnify')
anta = end, here: from . . . to
asya = his (from *idam*)
vaśīkāra = mastery (see I.15)

His mastery [extends] from the most minute to the greatest magnitude.

Contrary to the opinion of most translators, this aphorism does not extoll the supranatural powers attributed to the adept. It is merely an explication of the previous *sūtra*, and the 'mastery' spoken of simply refers to the *yogin's* ability to hold his mind stable in relation to any object irrespective of its size or type. In other words, those who are skilled in the art of concentration can achieve 'restriction' with regard to any of the myriads of cosmic forms.

I.41 *kṣīṇa-vṛtter-abhijātasya-iva maṇer-grahītṛ-grahaṇa-grāhyeṣu tat-stha-tad-añjanatā samāpattiḥ*

kṣīṇa = dwindled (from √*kṣi* 'to decrease')
vṛtti = fluctuation (see I.2)
abhijāta = precious, here: transparent (from *abhi* + √*jan* 'to beget')
iva = like
maṇi = jewel
grahītṛ = lit. 'grasper' (from √*grah* 'to seize' + *tṛ*)
grahaṇa = lit. 'grasping' (from √*grah* 'to seize')
grāhya = lit. 'grasped' (from √*grah*)
tad = that
stha = abide (from √*sthā* 'to stand')
tad = that
añjanatā = lit. 'anointment', here: anointed (from √*añj* 'to anoint' + *ana* + *tā*)
samāpatti = coincidence (from *sam* + *ā* + √*pat* 'to fall')

[In the case of a consciousness whose] fluctuations have dwindled [and which has become] like a transparent jewel, [there results]—[with reference to] the 'grasper', 'grasping' and the 'grasped'—[a state of] coincidence with that on which [consciousness] abides and by which [consciousness] is 'anointed'.

This is a description of the process of identification underlying the technique of enstasy (*samādhi*). Upon the complete restriction of all fluctuations, consciousness undergoes a profound transformation in which the experienced object (the 'grasped') and the experiencing subject (the 'grasper') become as it were identical. This is what is technically known as 'coincidence' or, in the language of the western mystics, *coincidentia oppositorum*. This mode of cognition reveals the essential nature (*sva-rūpa*) of the object of concentration, that is, the object as it is in itself. As the Persian mystic Jālāl-ud-din Rūmī exclaims: 'This is the greatest wonder, that thou and I, sitting here in the same nook, Are at this moment both in 'Irāq and Khorāsān, thou and I.'[8] In *samādhi* the boundaries of space and time which ordinarily separate one thing from another are abolished, and cognition becomes instant and immediate.

I.42 *tatra śabda-artha-jñāna-vikalpaiḥ saṃkīrṇā savitarkā samāpattiḥ*

tatra = in that (see I.13)
śabda = sound, here: word (see I.9)
artha = meaning, here: intent (see I.28)
jñāna = knowledge (see I.8)
vikalpa = imagination, here: conceptual (see I.9)
saṃkīrṇa = mixed, here: interspersed (from *sam* + √*kṝ* 'to scatter')
savitarka = cogitative, here: with cogitation (from *sa* + *vi* + √*tark* 'to reflect')
samāpatti = coincidence (see I.41)

[So long as there is] conceptual knowledge [based on] the intent of words in this [enstasy], [then this state is called] coincidence interspersed with cogitation.

When the process of subject-object identification occurs with reference to a 'coarse' (*sthūla*) object—i.e. a visible thing—and is accompanied by spontaneously arising presented-ideas (*pratyaya*), then this particular type of enstasy bears the technical designation

[8] Quoted in R. A. Nicholson (1975[3]), p. 168.

of 'cogitative coincidence'. What 'cogitation' (*vitarka*) consists in has already been explained (see I.17). The fact that such flashes of understanding with regard to the object of concentration can bubble up at all in enstasy bespeaks the incomplete degree of identification achieved. These presented-ideas are called 'cogitations' only in analogy to the ordinary thought processes which lack the former's immediacy and lucidity. There is no rambling of thoughts in *samādhi*, no vague conceptualisation, but these presented-ideas constitute spontaneous acts of insight or knowledge, which, although grounded in the concepts derived from ordinary experiencing, have a different quality or feel about them.

I.43 *smṛti-pariśuddhau sva-rūpa-śūnya-iva-artha-mātra-nirbhāsā nirvitarkā*

smṛti = memory, here: depth-memory (from √*smṛ* 'to recall')
pariśuddhi = purification (from *pari* + √*śudh* 'to purify')
sva = own, *rūpa* = form } here: essence
śūnya = void, here: empty (see I.9)
iva = as it were
artha = object (see I.28)
mātra = mere, here: only
nirbhāsa = shining forth (from *nir* + √*bhās* 'to be bright')
nirvitarkā = ultra-cogitative (from *nir* + *vi* + √*tark*)

On the purification of the depth-memory [which has become], as it were, empty of its essence, [and when] the object alone is shining forth—[then this state is called] ultra-cogitative [coincidence].

This aphorism describes the condition of complete 'coincidence' with regard to an object taken from the visible realm of nature. In this enstatic state no conceptualisation of any kind occurs. There *is* just the object. Identification is perfect, and it no longer makes any sense to ask whether the object is *in* the *yogin*'s consciousness or his consciousness is in the object. Subject and object have merged so completely that one cannot detect any seam. By 'purification of the depth-memory' is meant the temporary warding-off of those subliminal-activators which are responsible for the conceptualisation of experienced reality. The term *smṛti*, in the present context, does not stand for the 'fluctuation' mentioned in I.6; it clearly denotes the subconscious or, as I prefer to call it, the depth-memory. In *nirvitarka-samādhi* or ultra-cogitative enstasy all presented-ideas are restricted. This is a repetition, though on a higher level, of the same process that led to the restriction of the fluctuations in meditation. The *yogin* hopes that, by preventing the subliminal-activators from forming presented-ideas, the subconscious deposit will deplete itself, which is tantamount to Self-realisation or emancipation.

I.44 *etayā-eva savicārā nirvicārā ca sūkṣma-viṣayā vyākhyātā*

etayā = by this (from *etad* 'this')
eva = thus
savicāra = reflexive (from *sa* + *vi* + √*car* 'to move')
nirvicāra = ultra-reflexive (from *nir* + *vi* + √*car*)
ca = and
sūkṣma = subtle (from √*siv* 'to sew'?)
viṣaya = object (see I.11)
vyākhyāta = explained (from *vi* + *ā* + √*khyā* 'to be mentioned')

Thus by this [above-mentioned form of coincidence] [the other two types of enstasy]—[viz.] the reflexive and the ultra-reflexive—are explained; [these have] subtle objects [as props for concentration].

The process of enstatic identification is the same whether the object held in consciousness is of a 'coarse' (*sthūla*) or a 'subtle' (*sūkṣma*) nature. Conceptual activity in *samādhi* is called *vitarka* when it refers to objects of the former type and *vicāra* or 'reflection' when it concerns objects of the latter class. In both instances the fundamental task confronting the *yogin* is the same: to achieve complete identification with the object by carefully repelling all presented-ideas as soon as they emerge. When the mind's conceptualising tendency has been brought to a halt the resultant state of consciousness is known as 'ultra-cogitative' (*nirvitarka*) in regard to a coarse object and 'ultra-reflexive' (*nirvicāra*) when the object of identification belongs to the invisible realm of Nature.

I.45 *sūkṣma-viṣayatvaṃ ca-aliṅga-paryavasānam*

sūkṣma = subtle (see I.44)
viṣayatva = lit. 'objectness', here: object (see I.11)
ca = and
aliṅga = undifferentiate (from *a* + √*liṅg* 'to be attached to'; *liṅga* meaning 'mark, token')

paryavasāna = termination, here: terminate (from *pari* + *ava* + √*sā* (*san*) 'to gain')

And the subtle objects terminate in the Undifferentiate.

As I have explained in the Introduction (pp. 13f.), Nature (*prakṛti*) comprises two major dimensions or strata; one visible (broadly speaking), the other invisible. To the visible realm belong all material objects, the senses and also the 'surface' mind (*manas*). All other aspects of Nature pertain to the 'subtle' dimension of cosmic existence. This includes the transcendental core of the universe itself.

I.46 *tā eva sabījaḥ samādhiḥ*

tāḥ = these (from *tad*)
eva = verily
sabīja = with seed (from *sa* + *bīja* 'seed')
samādhi = enstasy (see I.20)

These [kinds of coincidence] verily [belong to the class of] enstasy with seed.

The four types of coincidence (*samāpatti*) mentioned above (I.42–4), viz. *savitarka, nirvitarka, savicāra* and *nirvicāra*, are characterised as enstasies 'with seed'. According to Vijñāna Bhikṣu these seeds are none other than the subliminal-activators from which springs the entire *conceptualised* universe. As long as they have not been eradicated, that is, burnt to ashes by the fire of the highest form of enstasy, the renewed occurrence of thought processes in *samādhi* and consequently the loss of the unmediated, non-conceptual mode of apprehension is an ever acute possibility. In Vyāsa's opinion the term *bīja* denotes merely the objective 'support' (*ālambana*) or the object of enstatic identification, but this interpretation leads to difficulties in understanding aphorism I.51.

I.47 *nirvicāra- vaiśāradye'adhyātma-prasādaḥ*

nirvicāra = ultra-reflexive (see I.44)
vaiśāradya = lucidity (from *vai* + *śarad* 'autumn'; meaning 'autumnal brightness')
adhyātman = peculiar to oneself, here: inner-being (from *adhi* + *ātma* 'self')
prasāda = pacification (cf. I.33: *prasādana*), here: clarity

When there is lucidity in the ultra-reflexive [enstasy], [then this is called] the clarity of the inner-being.

At the peak of the ultra-reflexive identification with a subtle object, consciousness reaches its greatest lucidity. This state is compared by Patañjali with the extraordinary brightness of the autumnal sky of northern India. It is statements and metaphors like this which clearly discredit those biased critics of Yoga who refuse to see in *samādhi* anything else but a condition of reduced awareness or even total unconsciousness. *Samādhi* means a state of supra-wakefulness in which the *yogin*, as Swami Nikhilananda once put it, 'comes face to face with the true nature of the object, which ordinarily remains hidden behind the outer form'.[9]

I.48 *ṛtaṃ-bharā tatra prajñā*

ṛta = truth (from √*ar* 'to fit' (?); meaning 'right, proper')
bharā = bearing (from √*bhṛ* 'to bear')
tatra = in that (see I.13)
prajñā = insight (from *pra* + √*jñā* 'to know')

In this [state of utmost lucidity] insight is truth-bearing.

In contradistinction to the piecemeal fashion in which all ordinary knowledge is acquired, the gnostic insight (*prajñā*) engendered in the highest degree of object-dependent enstasy comes in a 'flash' (*sphuṭa*) and is complete in itself and without any progression. It reveals the object in its essence (*tattva*) and for this reason is called 'truth-bearing', that is, genuinely infallible. The object is known as it is, once and for all, by way of unmediated pure apperception in which there is no room for error.

I.49 *śruta-anumāna-prajñābhyām-anya-viṣayā viśeṣa-arthatvāt*

śruta = lit. 'heard', here: tradition (from √*śru* 'to hear')
anumāna = inference (see I.7)
prajñā = insight (see I.48)
anya = other, here: distinct
viṣaya = object, here: scope (see I.11)
viśeṣa = special, here: particular (see I.22)
arthatva = purposiveness (from *artha* + *tva*)

The scope [of this gnostic insight] is distinct from the insight [gained from] tradition and inference [owing to its] particular purposiveness.

Vyāsa and the other Sanskrit exegetes interpret this aphorism somewhat differently. According to them the phrase *viśeṣa-arthatva*

[9] Swami Nikhilananda (1951), p. 95.

refers to the 'particularity' of a given object. Ordinary knowledge, derived from tradition (testimony) or inference, is said to deal only with the 'general', whereas the 'particular' is the proper domain of perception. For instance, a distinction has to be made between 'house' as a category concept and 'house' as a specific, or particular, object of perception. Gnostic insight is likened to perceptual knowledge which always grasps the 'particular', never the 'genus' of a thing. Although this philosophical interpretation is of course not wrong, an alternative explanation of the present *sūtra* is possible and at least equally credible. The word *arthatva* can also be understood in the sense of 'purpose' or rather 'purposiveness'. The 'special purpose' of that gnostic flash of insight could then be thought to lie in its bridging function between the empirical consciousness and the transcendental Self-awareness. Whereas ordinary conceptual knowledge keeps a person embroiled in the cosmic flux, the yogic *prajñā* is instrumental in effecting the *yogin*'s final exodus from prakṛtic or conditioned existence. It brings about deliverance from human bondage by setting up a counter-force which combats the deep-seated propensity of consciousness towards externalisation.

I.50 *taj-jah saṃskāro'nya-saṃskāra-pratibandhī*

tad = that
ja = born (from √*jan* 'to beget')
saṃskāra = subliminal-activator (see I.18)
anya = other
saṃskāra = subliminal-activator
pratibandhin = obstructing, here: obstructs (from *prati* + √*bandh* 'to bind')

The subliminal-activator born from that [gnostic flash] obstructs the other subliminal-activators.

The stepless gnosis of the *nirvicāra-vaiśāradya* enstasy generates, by virtue of the suspension of all presented-ideas (conceptual activity), a subliminal-activator which runs counter to the subliminal forces inherent in the depth-mind straining towards thought formation and the externalisation of consciousness. This perfect restriction of all mentation leads over into the condition of *asaṃprajñāta-samādhi*, in which pure Self-awareness is recovered.

I.51 *tasya-api nirodhe sarva-nirodhān-nirbījaḥ samādhiḥ*

tasya = its, here: of this (from *tad*)

api = also
nirodha = restriction (see I.2)
sarva = all
nirodha = restriction
nirbīja = seedless, here: without seed (from *nis* + *bīja*)
samādhi = enstasy (see I.20)

Upon the restriction also of this [regressive subliminal-activator][there ensues], owing to the restriction of all [contents of consciousness], the enstasy without seed.

Yoga is the progressive elimination of consciousness-of (*citta*) in order to secure pure Self-awareness. In *asaṃprajñāta-samādhi* only the subliminal 'deposit' of the empirical consciousness (or, in the language of the phenomenologists, of the consciousness-of) remains. As has already been explained in connection with aphorism I.18, the network of subliminal-activators is the dynamo responsible for the production of the various states of consciousness, and hence the last phase of the yogic process of involution must be the destruction of this subconscious web itself. But this is not an active undertaking on the part of the *yogin*, for this would presuppose an ego which is prior to the depth-mind. However, as we have seen, by the time the *yogin* reaches the state of *nirvicāra-vaiśāradya*, his consciousness has become virtually non-existent. Since the ego is a phenomenon closely bound up with the empirical consciousness, its elimination (or, better, transcendence) is implied by the abrogation of consciousness. The non-directed activity which occurs in the condition of ultra-cognitive enstasy may be compared with the happenings within a culture of antagonistic bacteria which gradually destroy each other. The sustained practice of *asaṃprajñāta-samādhi* spontaneously levels off the subconscious deposit and in due course brings about the terminal state of *nirbīja-samādhi* (see IV.29) where the Self (*puruṣa*), or root-consciousness, reveals itself. In the words of the author of the *Haṭhayoga-Pradīpikā* (IV.62): 'Upon the abandonment of the objects of knowledge the mind becomes dissolved. Upon the dissolution of the mind [all that] remains is the aloneness [of the Self].'

Perfection in Yoga is not achieved by mere reading of the scriptures.
Haṭhayoga-Pradīpikā I.65[b]

Chapter Two
SĀDHANA-PĀDA

spiritual practice

Note: The word *sādhana* means 'path-to-realisation' which sums up the contents of the second chapter quite well. Of course, various means of attaining the transformation of consciousness into pure Self-awareness have been expounded already in the introductory chapter, and it is probable that these chapter headings are the work of a copyist rather than the original author. As I have explained elsewhere,[10] the second book is a composite of two independent traditions, viz. the Kriyā-Yoga of Patañjali and the *aṣṭa-aṅga-yoga* of whose systematic model Patañjali availed himself. The aphorisms belonging to the latter tradition appear to be *quoted* in the main body of the *Yoga-Sūtra*, and it is certainly one of the curious vicissitudes of history that today Patañjali's name should be so consistently associated with the 'eightfold path' and not with the philosophically grounded Kriyā-Yoga originally developed by him. Introducing the second chapter, Vācaspati Miśra makes this observation: 'In the first chapter practice and dispassion were given out as the means of Yoga. However, as these two do not come into being instantaneously for one [whose consciousness] is emergent, he is in need of the means taught in the second chapter in order to purify the *sattva*.'

II.1 *tapaḥ svādhyāya-īśvara-praṇidhānāni kriyā-yogaḥ*

tapas = self-castigation, here: ascesis (from √*tap* 'to be hot'; lit. meaning 'heat')
svādhyāya = self-study (from *sva* 'own' + *adhi* + *ā* + √*i* 'to go'; lit. meaning 'one's going into')

[10] See G. Feuerstein (1979).

īśvara = lord (see I.23)
praṇidhāna = devotion (see I.23)
kriyā = action (from √*kṛ* 'to do')
yoga = (see I.1)

Ascesis, self-study and devotion to the Lord [constitute] Kriyā-Yoga.

Whereas aphorism I.2 defines the initial phase of the yogic process of internalisation, the present *sūtra* names the three cardinal techniques of Patañjali's Yoga. As I have pointed out already, Kriyā-Yoga is not a mere preliminary ritual to the practice of the so-called 'eightfold Yoga', but it forms a full-fledged tradition of its own which, moreover, must be understood as Patañjali's teaching proper. This raises the question as to the precise relation between the categories of 'practice' and 'dispassion' on the one hand and the triple means of Kriyā-Yoga on the other. The following diagram may prove useful here:

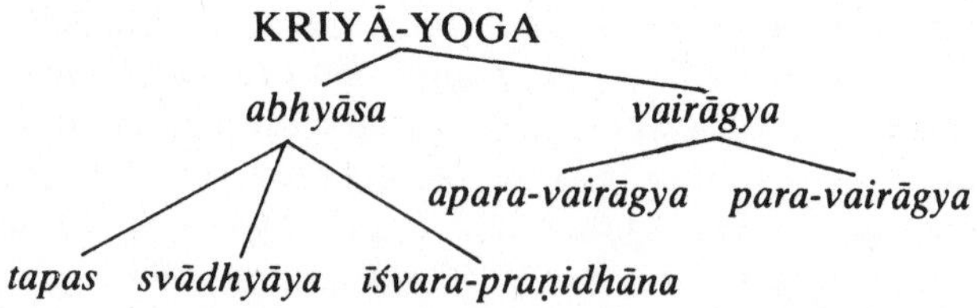

As can be seen from this tree diagram, *abhyāsa* and *vairāgya* or 'practice' and 'dispassion' represent the most comprehensive categories. Whereas 'dispassion' consists of two forms, viz. relative or incomplete renunciation and absolute renunciation taking place in the higher degree of enstasy, the category of 'practice' subsumes the three means of Kriyā-Yoga. From this follows that, contrary to popular opinion, *tapas* does not refer to any specific exercise but is, like *abhyāsa* and *vairāgya*, a formal category. It can be said to comprise all those exercises which fall outside the categories of 'self-study' and 'devotion to the Lord'.

The *aṣṭa-aṅga* tradition offers a different systematisation of the components of the yogic path, where the well-known eight members—not stages—are preferably to be considered as sub-categories of *abhyāsa*.

II.2 *samādhi-bhāvana-arthaḥ kleśa-tanū-karaṇa-arthaś-ca*
samādhi = enstasy (see I.20)

bhāvana = cultivation, here: cultivating (from √*bhū* 'to become')
artha = object, meaning, here: purpose (see I.28)
kleśa = cause-of-affliction (see II.1)
tanū = fine } here: attenuating
karaṇa = making (from √*kṛ* 'to do') } here: attenuating
artha = purpose (see I.28)
ca = and

[This Yoga has] the purpose of cultivating enstasy as also the purpose of attenuating the causes-of-affliction.

The central objective of Kriyā-Yoga is the gradual transformation of consciousness by means of meditative-absorption (*dhyāna*) and enstasy (*samādhi*). Progress in Yoga is, above all, dependent upon the cultivation of the enstatic mode of consciousness which is the only avenue to Self-realisation. Vācaspati Miśra observes that Kriyā-Yoga can bring about the attenuation but not the complete abolition of the causes-of-affliction; the latter, he argues, is achieved by means of the enstatic state of *prasaṃkhyāna* or 'elevation' (see IV.29), which is a particular phase of *asaṃprajñāta-samādhi*. This, again, is meant to emphasise that the occurrence of the ultra-cognitive mode of consciousness cannot be forced by any yogic technique, but comes about spontaneously and autonomously. All the *yogin* can do is to prepare himself for this radical transmutation as best he can. It is not subservient to his will and for this reason has very frequently been interpreted in terms of an act of grace (*prasāda*).

That Kriyā-Yoga is not designed for an Olympiad of enstatic tricks, but that it serves a higher purpose, is clear from the additional qualification that it is intended to attenuate the causes-of-affliction and thereby to eradicate nescience (*avidyā*) which is synonymous with the extirpation of the sub-consciousness.

II.3 *avidyā-asmitā-rāga-dveṣa-abhiniveśāḥ pañca-kleśāḥ*

avidyā = nescience (from *a* + √*vid* 'to know')
asmitā = lit. 'I-am-ness' (see I.17)
rāga = attachment (see I.37)
dveṣa = aversion (from √*dviṣ* 'to dislike')
abhiniveśa = will-to-live (from *abhi* + *ni* + √*viś* 'to dwell')
pañca = five
kleśa = cause-of-affliction (see I.24)

Nescience, I-am-ness, attachment, aversion and the will-to-live are the five causes-of-affliction.

The theory of the causes-of-affliction is, as I. K. Taimni correctly notes, 'the foundation of the system of *Yoga* outlined by Patañjali'.[11] We have encountered this key concept in connection with two previous aphorisms (viz. I.5 and I.24). What exactly are these factors which keep man ensconced in conditional or prakṛtic existence? Patañjali supplies some useful definitions which will help us to make better sense of this intriguing theory.

II.4 *avidyā kṣetram-uttareṣāṃ prasupta-tanu-vicchinna-udārāṇām*

avidyā = nescience (see I.3)
kṣetra = field (from √*kṣi* 'to inhabit')
uttara = other
prasupta = dormant (from *pra* + √*svap* 'to sleep')
tanu = lit. 'thin', here: attenuated (from √*tan* 'to stretch out')
vicchinna = lit. 'cut off', here: intercepted (from *vi* + √*chid* 'to cut')
udāra = aroused (from *ud* + √*ṛ* 'to move')

Nescience is the field of the other [causes-of-affliction]; [they can be] dormant, attenuated, intercepted or aroused.

The primary *kleśa*, the 'breeding ground' of the other four types, is nescience. This is not to be understood as a mere lack of knowledge; it is the absence of Self-awareness and thus, positively, false knowledge, distorted cognition. *Avidyā* is the cause of the fatal epistemic dichotomisation into subject and object which Yoga seeks to remove. *Avidyā* conceals the root-consciousness by establishing a false identity.

The causes-of-affliction are said to exist in four operational modes. They can be:

(1) *prasupta* or dormant, in the shape of the subconscious deposit (*āśaya*) of subliminal-activators;
(2) *tanu* or attenuated, that is restricted in their activity by means of yogic practices;
(3) *vicchinna* or intercepted, as when one type of *kleśa* temporarily blocks the operation of another;
(4) *udāra* or aroused, that is, fully active.

[11] I. K. Taimni (1961), p. 130.

II.5 *anitya-aśuci-duḥkha-anātmasu nitya-śuci-sukha-ātma-khyātir-avidyā*

anitya = ephemeral (from *a* + *ni* + *tya*)
aśuci = impure (from *a* + √*śuc* 'to glow')
duḥkha = sorrowful (see I.31)
anātman = non-self (from *an* + *ātman*)
nitya = eternal (see above)
śuci = pure (see above)
sukha = joyful (see I.33)
ātman = self (etymology uncertain: ? *tman* 'vital breath')
khyāti = vision, here: seeing (see I.16)
avidyā = nescience (see II.3)

Nescience is the seeing of [that which is] eternal, pure, joyful and the Self in [that which is] ephemeral, impure, sorrowful and the non-self.

Nescience is a cognitive error, a mistaken conviction about one's identity, which is congenital to man. Socialisation and education reinforce his innate belief in a false self, and it is only when he becomes aware of the pervasive social and cultural mechanisms which create and sustain his erroneous self image that he can begin to resist them and set out to discover his true identity, which is the Self (*puruṣa*).

II.6 *dṛg-darśana-śaktyor-eka-ātmatā-iva-asmitā*

dṛś = seer, here: vision-er (from √*dṛś* 'to see')
darśana = seeing, here: vision (see I.30)
śakti = power (from √*śak* 'to be able')
eka = one } here: identification
ātmatā = lit. 'self-ness' }
iva = as it were
asmitā = I-am-ness (see I.17)

I-am-ness is the identification as it were of the powers of vision and 'vision-er' [i.e. the Self].

Nescience is a fundamental category error which regards the Self as other than what it really is, and this leads to the active malidentification of the root-consciousness (Self) with consciousness (*citta*). In other words, we are all born in ignorance of our true nature and with the natural tendency of establishing our identity *outside* ourselves. At the bottom of all our endeavours at self-making (personality growth) and self-expression lies what Patañjali calls 'I-am-ness' (*asmitā*), the principle of individuation which is the product of nescience.

II.7 *sukha-anuśayī rāgaḥ*

sukha = pleasant (see I.33)
anuśayin = following, here: rest on (from *anu* + √*śī* 'to rest')
rāga = attachment (see I.37)

Attachment is [that which] rests on pleasant [experiences].

Having become identified with a particular organism and psychomental apparatus, we react to our environment in two principal ways. We feel, in varying gradation, either attracted or repelled, depending on the nature and quality of the experiences we make. There is an echo of the Freudian pleasure principle in this formulation. However, Patañjali's model admits of a third possibility which effectively disarms the accusation that he propounds a hedonistic psychology, viz. the transcendence of both attachment and displeasure.

II.8 *duḥkha-anuśayī dveṣaḥ*

duḥkha = sorrowful (see I.31)
anuśayin = following, here: rest on (see II.7)
dveṣa = aversion (see II.3)

Aversion is [that which] rests on sorrowful [experiences].

Attraction and aversion characterise man's general modes of relating to his environment. Of course, pleasure and displeasure/pain/sorrow are relative experiences, and hence what may be a pleasurable experience to one person can quite feasibly be painful or abhorrent to another. Ultimately, however, all is suffused with sorrow (see II.15). Patañjali affirms that a third response is open to man, which is the dispassionate attitude nurtured by the *yogin*.

II.9 *sva-rasa-vāhī viduṣo'pi tathā-rūḍho'bhiniveśaḥ*

sva = own
rasa = relish, inclination (from √*ras* 'to taste') } here: own-momentum
vāhin = bearing, flowing on (from √*vah* 'to flow')
vidvāṃs = knowing one (from √*vid* 'to know'), here: sage
api = also, here: even
tathā = thus

rūḍha = rooted (from √*ruh* 'to grow')
abhiniveśa = will-to-live (see II.3)

The will-to-live, flowing along [by its] own-momentum, is rooted thus even in the sages.

This aphorism describes the last of the five causes-of-affliction, the will-to-live, which is the basic drive for self-preservation inherent in every living being, including the wise men. All five *kleśas* are interdependent and mutually reinforce each other.

II.10 *te pratiprasava-heyāḥ sūkṣmāḥ*

te = they, here: these (see I.30)
pratiprasava = counter-flow, here: process-of-involution (from *prati* + *pra* + √*sū* 'to set in motion')
heya = to be overcome (from √*hā* 'to leave, abandon')
sūkṣma = subtle (see I.44)

These [causes-of-affliction], [in their] subtle [form], are to be overcome by the process-of-involution.

The causes-of-affliction are the factors responsible for man's construction and maintenance of a false identity, and they alienate him from the Self. Constituting an integral part of his very nature, how can he possibly hope to escape their dynamics? Patañjali gives a clear directive: Man can free himself by way of a radical reversal proceeding on two levels. The *kleśas*, he explains, have a subtle form and a coarse (*sthūla*) aspect. The former comprises first of all the subliminal-activators and, secondly, the presented-ideas as encountered in enstasy. The latter refers to the well-known fluctuations (*vṛtti*). The subliminal-activators can be destroyed by means of what he calls the process-of-involution or *pratiprasava*, which is the dissolving of consciousness as achieved through the prolonged practice of the various stages of enstasy. According to the cosmology of Yoga, the universe as we know it has evolved in a series of distinct stages commencing with the undifferentiated world ground (*prakṛti-pradhāna*). This evolutionary process is also known as *sarga* or *prasarga* both meaning 'creation'. In contrast to this, *pratiprasava* is the gradual involution of the *yogin's* personal cosmos, which ends in the flowing back of the primary-constituents (*guṇa*) into the primal cosmic matrix. Clearly, the *yogin* must begin with the more external aspect of the causes-of-affliction, namely the fluctuations, as is explained in the next aphorism.

II.11 *dhyāna-heyās-tad-vṛttayaḥ*

dhyāna = meditative-absorption (see I.39)
heya = to be overcome (see II.10)
tad = that, here: of these
vṛtti = fluctuation (see I.2)

The fluctuations of these [causes-of-affliction] are to be overcome by meditative-absorption.

This concise aphorism deserves our full attention since it unequivocally refutes the assertion found in some of the commentaries that the fluctuations are eliminated through the practice of enstasy. In fact, their stoppage is an essential precondition for the occurrence of the enstatic consciousness. Whatever cognitive elements are to be met with in the enstatic frame of mind, they are definitely not of the nature of the *vṛttis*.

II.12 *kleśa-mūlaḥ karma-āśayo dṛṣṭa-adṛṣṭa-janma-vedanīyaḥ*

kleśa = cause-of-affliction (see I.24)
mūla = root (from √*mūr* 'to become rigid')
karman = action (see I.24)
āśaya = deposit (see I.24)
dṛṣṭa = seen (see I.15)
adṛṣṭa = unseen (see I.15)
janman = birth (from √*jan* 'to beget')
vedanīya = to be experienced (from √*vid* 'to know, be conscious of')

The causes-of-affliction are the root of the action-deposit, and [this] may be experienced in the seen [i.e. present] birth or in an unseen [i.e. future] [birth].

The causes-of-affliction are not unlike the 'drives' of earlier psychologists. They are thought to prompt the individual to act, sociate, feel, think and assert himself and thereby repeatedly to affirm and consolidate his self-image as a finite entity other than the transcendental Self. This world involvement under the false identity of a distinct, spatio-temporal individuality leads to the piling up of subconscious deposit (*āśaya*) which, in turn, impels man to renewed action and experience. We thus get the following vicious cycle:

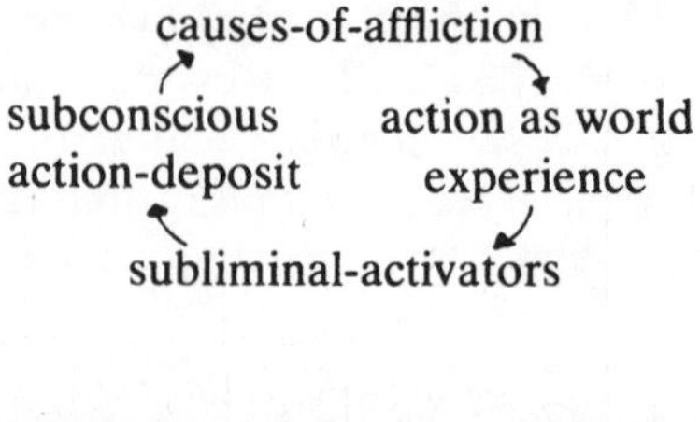

This is an analytical version of the mythological wheel of becoming (*bhava-cakra*), the circle of conditioned existence or *saṃsāra*. This existential cycle encompasses, as is evident from the present aphorism, not only the current embodiment, but all future lives of a person. The notion of reincarnation, or repeated births, is one of the main pillars of almost all branches of Indian thought, and Patañjali unquestioningly adopts it as one of the axioms of his philosophy. Whatever one makes of this metaphysical conception, it is of no immediate relevance to the actual practice of Kriyā-Yoga whose tacit objective is the disruption of the existential cycle in *this* life.

The dynamics of re-embodiment is thought to operate on the simple formula that meritorious action results in subliminal-activators of a positive quality leading to emotionally pleasant experiences in life, whereas demeritorious actions produce subliminal-activators of a negative sort which have adverse results in the person's life. This is the iron law of moral retribution. In other words, the structures in the depth-mind, inherited from a previous embodiment, have a regulative function in the individual's present incarnation without, however, determining the precise nature and content of his experiences. Vācaspati Miśra, in his gloss on aphorism II.15, offers an interesting model of the way in which subconscious impulses and overt behaviour interlink:

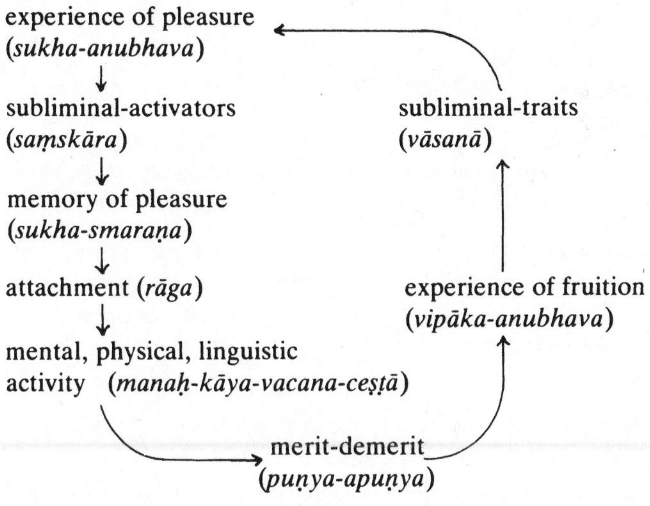

II.13 *sati mūle tad-vipāko jāty-āyur-bhogāḥ*

sati = being, here: exists (from √*as* 'to be')

mūla = root (see II.12)
tad = that, here: from it
vipāka = fruition (see I.24)
jāti = birth (from √*jan* 'to beget')
āyus = life, here: span-of-life (from *ā* + √*i* 'to go')
bhoga = experience, enjoyment (from √*bhuj* 'to enjoy')

[So long as] the root exists, [there is also] fruition from it: birth, life and enjoyment.

Vyāsa introduces a pertinent simile: 'Just as the grains of rice, encased within the chaff, are capable of germination . . . unlike the winnowed chaff or burnt seed . . . so also the action-deposits, encased in the causes-of-affliction, are capable of fruition, but not the winnowed causes-of-affliction.' The so-called fruition of the causes-of-affliction is threefold inasmuch as they determine the birth, the span of individual existence and its content or experience. Naturally, this determinacy cannot be all-comprehensive; otherwise there would be no scope for asserting one's will to break out of this cycle.

II.14 *te hlāda-paritāpa-phalāḥ puṇya-apuṇya-hetutvāt*

te = they, here: these (see I.30)
hlāda = delight (from √*hlād* 'to rejoice')
paritāpa = distress (from *pari* + √*tap* 'to be hot, distressed')
phala = fruit, here: result (from √*phal* 'to ripen, bear fruit')
puṇya = meritorious (see I.33)
apuṇya = demeritorious (see I.33)
hetutva = lit. 'causality', here: cause (from *hetu*, see II.17)

These [three] have delight or distress as results, according to the causes, [which may be] meritorious or demeritorious.

The over-all quality of birth, life and life experiences of an individual is determined by the quality of the stock of subliminal-activators which constitute the *résumé* as it were of that person's previous embodiment(s).

II.15 *pariṇāma-tāpa-saṃskāra-duḥkhair-guṇa-vṛtti-virodhāc-ca duḥkham-eva sarvaṃ vivekinaḥ*

pariṇāma = transformation (from *pari* + √*nam* 'to bend')
tāpa = anguish (see II.14)
saṃskāra = subliminal-activator (see I.18)
duḥkha = sorrow (see I.31)

guṇa = primary-constituent (see I.16)
vṛtti = fluctuation, here: movement (see I.2)
virodha = conflict (from *vi* + √*rudh* 'to stop')
ca = and
duḥkha = sorrow (see I.31)
eva = thus, here: merely, but
sarva = all
vivekin = discerner (from *vi* + √*vic* 'to examine, discern')

Because of the sorrow in the [continual] transformation [of the world-ground], [in] the anguish [and in] the subliminal-activators and on account of the conflict between the movements of the primary-constituents—to the discerner all is but sorrow.

In the previous aphorism, as also in II.6 and II.7, Patañjali affirmed the possibility of agreeable or pleasurable experiences. Now he shifts his stance and proposes an analysis of world experience which is more penetrating than the simple pleasure/displeasure model of common-sense. He, in fact, argues that the experiences of pleasure, joy, happiness, are all deceptive. In truth, life is sorrowful. He does not, as we have seen, deny that we can experience moments of pleasure. But by casting his net much wider than does non-philosophical understanding, he shows that the very impermanence of pleasure is itself experienced as sorrowful.

Nature is continually transforming itself and offers man no foothold. Change is the very essence of conditioned existence. Our need for security is therefore destined to remain unfulfilled. Below the surface of pleasant or unpleasant experiences lie a basic anxiety and anguish which are common to all men—an insight which contemporary existentialism and the psychotherapeutic schools of thought have rediscovered for the twentieth century. Yoga and Indian philosophy in general have frequently been accused of pessimism on account of statements like the above generalisation of sorrow. That this criticism is totally unfounded can be seen from the next aphorism. At the same time, this unmasking of our transient experiences of pleasure as essentially sorrowful will also defend Yoga against the charge of selfish hedonism.

II.16 *heyaṃ duḥkham-anāgatam*
heya = to be overcome (see II.10)
duḥkha = sorrow (see I.31)

anāgata = non-present, future, here: yet-to-come (from *an* + *ā* + √*gam* 'to go')

[That which is] to be overcome is sorrow yet-to-come.

A. J. Bahm translates this important prescription flatly with 'It is possible to avoid future evil.' Patañjali is far more decided. For him, the conquest of sorrow is not only possible but a challenge which ought to be taken up. To the *yogin*, who, as Vyāsa says, has become as sensitive as an eye-ball, it is imperative to end all self-deception in order to reach the Self. For the Self is the ultimate security. Standing beyond the perpetual change of the finite cosmos, the Self alone is unaffected by any sorrow, anguish or pain. But how is future sorrow to be prevented?

II.17 *draṣṭṛ-dṛśyayoḥ saṃyogo heya-hetuḥ*

draṣṭṛ = seer (see I.3)
dṛśya = the seen (from √*dṛś* 'to see')
saṃyoga = correlation (from *sam* + √*yuj* 'to yoke, join')
heya = to be overcome (see II.10)
hetu = reason, here: cause (from √*hi* 'to incite')

The correlation between the seer [i.e. the Self] and the seen [i.e. Nature] is the cause [of that which is] to be overcome.

Sorrow, explains Patañjali, is the inevitable result of man's mistaken identity, his 'fall' from the Self. The correlation between the root-consciousness and the objective world (including the psycho-mental processes) is not a substantive merging or coming into contact, for both entities are forever separate. It is merely an *apparent*—and essentially enigmatic—relation. It is a *given* in human experience and ultimately inexplicable in empirical terms. The Self is characterised as the 'seer' (*draṣṭṛ*) or the 'power of awareness' (*cit-śakti*), whereas the world, in its unmanifest and manifest form, is that which is seen by the seer. This strange relation is also circumscribed by the technical term *saṃnidhi* or 'proximity'. As Vācaspati Miśra (I.4) puts it: 'The consciousness (*citta*) is not linked to the Self, but is proximate to it. And this proximity does not result from a spatial or temporal connection of the Self with that [consciousness]. Rather, the characteristic [of this proximity] is a [certain] "capacity" (*yogyatā*)'. In other words, no external relationship is involved but an internal fitness; namely, the capacity of the Self to apperceive, and the capacity of the world to be apperceived. Another way of explaining this abstruse philosophical doctrine is by means of the metaphor of reflection (*pratibimba*), as developed by Vācaspati Miśra. Here the Self is said to be mirrored in the empirical consciousness and this reflected 'light' of the Self then makes contact with the objective world. However, this is hardly any more satisfactory than the other solutions to the problem of how two eternally distinct entities can ever become entangled with each other. But Patañjali has made his philosophical commitment to dualism, and we must suspend our judgement on this theoretical issue for the time being in order to appreciate the practical solution proposed by him.

II.18 *prakāśa-kriyā-sthiti-śīlaṃ bhūta-indriya-ātmakaṃ bhoga-apavarga-arthaṃ dṛśyam*

prakāsa = brightness (from *pra* + √*kāś* 'to be visible')
kriyā = action, here: activity (see II.1)
sthiti = steadiness, here: inertia (see I.13)
śīla = character
bhūta = element (from √*bhū* 'to become')
indriya = instrument, here: sense-organ (from *indra* + *ya*)
ātmaka = having the nature of, here: embodied in (from *ātman* + *ka*)
bhoga = enjoyment (see II.13)
apavarga = emancipation (from *apa* + √*vṛj* 'to turn away')
artha = object, here: purpose (see I.28)
dṛśya = the seen (see II.17)

The seen [i.e. Nature] has the character of brightness, activity and inertia; it is embodied in elements and sense-organs [and it serves] the [dual] purpose of enjoyment and emancipation.

As Max Müller noted long ago, 'Indian philosophers have the excellent habit of always explaining the meaning of their technical terms.'[12] This certainly applies to Patañjali. The present and the next aphorism proffer a definition of the important term *dṛśya*. We are told that it denotes everything that is capable of becoming the object of the transcendental subject or Self, that is to say, the entire body of *prakṛti* including its causal core. The three principal modes of manifestation (*śīla*) are a clear reference to the interdependent activity of the primary-constituents (*guṇa*). 'Brightness' corresponds with *sattva*, 'activity' with *rajas* and 'inertia' with *tamas*. These three forms of appearance apply to the world of things as much as to the phenomena of consciousness. Nature (*prakṛti*), as I

[12] M. Müller (1916^4), p. 338.

have explained already, is a multidimensional structure whose most differentiated level is composed of the material elements (*bhūta*) and the sensory apparatus (*indriya*) of sentient organisms. We learn, moreover, that the world serves the dual purpose of experience and emancipation. This means that the 'seen' is the basis of either the Self's involvement in the processes of mundane existence or its withdrawal from all worldly activity. Strictly speaking, liberation and bondage pertain to the finite mind and are mistakenly attributed to the Self which is by definition always free. Liberation and bondage are thus merely intra-prakṛtic phenomena.

II.19 *viśeṣa-aviśeṣa-liṅga-mātra-aliṅgāni guṇa-parvāṇi*

viśeṣa = special, here: the particularised (see I.22)
aviśeṣa = here: the unparticularised (see I.22)
liṅga = mark, characteristic (from √*liṅg* 'to attach oneself')
mātra = only, mere } here:
aliṅga = the undifferentiate } the undifferentiate
guṇa = primary-constituent (see I.16)
parvan = level (from √*pṛ* 'to fill')

The levels of the primary-constituents are the particularised, the unparticularised, the differentiate and the undifferentiate.

The material elements and sense-receptors spoken of in the preceding aphorism are only a thin slice of the total reality of Nature. They belong to the level of the particularised. There are other, deeper levels of diminishing differentiation. This multi-level structuring of the cosmos has been delineated in the Introduction (pp. 13f.). Here I merely wish to point out that I. K. Taimni's attempt to link up these four levels with the vedāntic conception of the four 'envelopes' (*kośa*) is fallacious. Equally forced is the following correlation proposed by him:

vitarka-samādhi—viśeṣa
vicāra-samādhi—aviśeṣa
ānanda-samādhi—liṅga
asmitā-samādhi—aliṅga

According to the evidence of the *Yoga-Sūtra*, *vicāra-samādhi* covers the whole 'subtle' dimension of Nature (see I.45) and is therefore not confined to *aviśeṣa*. Furthermore, as I have indicated in my comments to I.17, it is highly unlikely that *ānanda* (joy) and *asmitā* (I-am-ness) constitute particular types of enstasy, at least not according to the schema adopted by Patañjali.

II.20 *draṣṭā dṛśi-mātraḥ śuddho'pi pratyaya-anupaśyaḥ*

draṣṭṛ = seer (see I.3)
dṛśi = seeing (from √*dṛś* 'to see')
mātra = only, here: sheer
śuddha = pure (from √*śudh* 'to purify')
api = also, here: although
pratyaya = presented-idea (see I.10)
anupaśya = behold, here: apperceive (from *anu* + √*paś* 'to see')

The seer [which is] the sheer [power of] seeing, although pure, apperceives the presented-ideas.

The seer is, as we know, the Self or root-consciousness. It is the transcendental subject which is said to 'apperceive' the 'perceptions' or presented-ideas of the empirical consciousness. It is important to distinguish carefully between the Self's apperception and the mind's perception. Whereas the perceptions of consciousness are related to objects outside consciousness (which may be actual or memorised objects), the apperception of the Self is related to the cognitions of consciousness and does not involve any extraneous factors. In other words, for the Self the ordinary consciousness presents itself as the object. Whilst the perceptions or cognitions of consciousness are multiple and discontinuous, the Self's apperception is perfectly continuous.

II.21 *tad-artha eva dṛśyasya-ātmā*

tad = that, here: this
artha = object, purpose, here: for the sake of (see I.28)
eva = verily, here: only
dṛśya = the seen (see II.17)
ātman = self, here: essence (see II.5)

The essence of the seen is only for the sake of this [seer].

If we ask for the ultimate significance of the world, we are given a definite and positive answer: The universe has, metaphysically speaking, meaning only insofar as it serves the Self's experience or liberation (see II.18). Beyond that it is of no relevance. On the other hand, the Self serves no purpose whatsoever, but is the highest goal of human aspiration so long as man still stands under the spell of nescience.

II.22 *kṛta-arthaṃ prati naṣṭam-apy-anaṣṭaṃ tad-anya-sādhāraṇatvāt*

kṛta = done, here: accomplished (from √*kṛ* 'to do') } here: whose purpose has been accomplished
artha = object, here: purpose
prati = with regard to, here: for
naṣṭa = ceased (from √*naś* 'to perish')
api = also, but, here: nevertheless
anaṣṭa = not ceased (see above)
tad = that, here: it
anya = other
sādhāraṇatva = communality, here: common-experience (from *sa* + *ā* + √*dhṛ* 'to hold' + *na* + *tva*)

Although [the seen] has ceased [to exist] for [the *yogin* whose] purpose has been accomplished, it has nevertheless not ceased [to exist altogether], since it is common-experience [with respect to all] other [beings].

This aphorism is as plain a refutation of mentalism as one can expect. The world is not a mere thought product which dissolves upon liberation. Objects are external to the mind and have their independent existence which is not affected by the event of Self-realisation. Emancipation is an individual achievement which abolishes man's false organismic identity and re-locates him into the Self. With the destruction of the consciousness complex the possibility of perceiving the external world, or perceiving the world externally, is likewise eliminated. But this absence of empirical perception does not conjure away the universe. It remains as real as before and continues to be experienced by those who erroneously identify not with the transcendental Self but with the phenomenal consciousness of a particular organism in space and time. Without this ontological assumption of the reality of the objective universe the emancipation of the very first liberated being would, logically, have entailed the annihilation of the cosmos and, by further implication, it would also have meant the emancipation of all other beings.

II.23 *sva-svāmi-śaktyoḥ sva-rūpa-upalabdhi-hetuḥ saṃyogaḥ*

sva = own, here: the owned
svāmin = owner (from *sva*)
śakti = power (see II.6)
sva = own
rūpa = form
upalabdhi = apprehension (from *upa* + √*labh* 'to obtain')
hetu = cause, here: reason (see II.17)

saṃyoga = correlation (see II.17)

The correlation [between the seer and the seen] is the reason for the apprehension of the own-form of the power of the owner and that of the owned.

This succinct technical statement is less obscure than it sounds. Patañjali merely reaffirms here that it is in virtue of the correlation between the Self and the non-self (i.e. Nature) that the essential nature of the Self and of the non-self can be grasped. In other words, metaphysics which points the way to the Self is possible only because of the apparent association of the transintelligible subject with a specific consciousness. It follows that when the Self has been recovered as it were, metaphysical thinking becomes not only unnecessary but impossible. The terms 'owner' and 'owned', referring to Self and world respectively, epitomise well the peculiar relation which exists between these two entities.

II.24 *tasya hetur-avidyā*

tasya = of this (from *tad*)
hetu = reason, here: cause (see II.17)
avidyā = nescience (see II.3)

The cause of this [correlation] is nescience.

This aphorism takes us back to the initial discussion of the second chapter, namely the practical consideration of the psychological reasons for man's spiritual degeneracy and his concomittant exposure to anxiety, distress, sorrow and pain. Nescience conceals man's true nature from himself and simultaneously compels him to assume a false identity ('I am such and such, possess such and such', etc.). Philosophically speaking, the Self becomes seemingly correlated with the non-self (consciousness and the objective world). Yet this linkage is not illusory but a very real experience of the finite mind.

II.25 *tad-abhāvāt saṃyoga-abhāvo hānaṃ tad-dṛśeḥ kaivalyam*

tad = that, here: this
abhāva = disappearance (see I.10)
saṃyoga = correlation (see II.17)
abhāva = disappearance (see I.10), here: disappear
hāna = cessation (from √*hā* 'to leave')
tad = that, here: this
dṛśi = seeing (see II.20)
kaivalya = aloneness (from *kevala* 'alone')

With the disappearance of this [nescience] the correlation [also] disappears; this is [total] cessation, the aloneness of the [sheer power of] seeing.

When nescience is dispelled, the correlation is likewise terminated. The result is total cessation of all consciousness and bodily activity. This supreme condition is also known as the 'aloneness of seeing', which is the pure subjectivity of the root-consciousness. The phrase 'aloneness of seeing' has not always been understood properly. It does not mean 'isolation of the seer' (J. H. Woods) or 'liberation of the seer' (I. K. Taimni). Rather it refers to the Self's capacity for continuous apperception, or seeing, when that apperception is without any presented-ideas, that is, 'alone'. Hence *kaivalya* is not simply a synonym of *mokṣa*, *mukti* or *apavarga* (see II.18).

II.26 *viveka-khyātir-aviplavā hāna-upāyaḥ*

viveka = discernment (see II.15)
khyāti = vision (see I.16)
aviplava = permanent, unceasing (from *avi* + √*plu* 'to swim, be transient')
hāna = cessation (see II.25)
upāya = means (from *upa* + √*i* 'to go')

The means of [attaining] cessation is the unceasing vision of discernment.

Consciousness is the product of the correlation between Self and world. The essence of Patañjali's Yoga can be said to consist in the separation (*viyoga*) of these two realities. Paradoxically, this can only be brought about through the finite consciousness itself. Thus the *yogin* disunites himself from the larger physical and social environment, from his own organism and even from his own mental processes, and thereby gradually steps back behind the multiple identities which man assumes in his everyday existence. This process is narried on even more acutely on the level of enstatic experiencing (in *samādhi*). Here the *yogin* deliberately identifies with the inner nature of a chosen object in order to loosen up for the ultimate practice of total withdrawal from all projected identities. At the height of enstasy, when consciousness is completely emptied of all contents but possesses awareness of its rarefied existence, the *yogin* must realise—and apply—the distinction between this vacated consciousness and the transcendental root-consciousness. This is known as the vision of discernment which effectively helps him to remove the last veil of nescience and to establish the identity of the Self. However, for Self-realisation to occur, even this exalted state of consciousness must naturally be abandoned (see III.50). The vision of discernment, it must be emphasised, is not a type of presented-idea. Rather it is the immediate certainty of the consciousness of its own existence as consciousness. The vision of discernment (*viveka-khyāti*) is, properly speaking, the terminal phase of *asaṃprajñāta-samādhi.*

II.27 *tasya saptadhā prānta-bhūmiḥ prajñā*

tasya = of it (from *tad*), here: for him
saptadha = sevenfold (from *sapta* 'seven' + *dha*)
prānta = last (from *pra* + *anta* 'end')
bhūmi = level, here: stage (see I.14)
prajñā = knowledge, here: transcendental-insight (see I.20)

For him [who possesses this unceasing vision of discernment] there arises, in the last stage, transcendental-insight [which is] sevenfold.

The gnostic insight spoken of here must not be confounded with the recurrence of presented-ideas. Patañjali merely wishes to explicate the central features implicit in this ultimate transcendence of consciousness. According to Vyāsa, the seven aspects of this gnosis are the following:

(1) that which is to be prevented, viz. future suffering, has been successfully identified;
(2) the causes of suffering have been eliminated once and for all;
(3) through the enstasy of restriction complete cessation has been achieved;
(4) the means of cessation, viz. the vision of discernment, has been applied;
(5) sovereignty of the depth-consciousness (*buddhi* = *sattva*) has been achieved;
(6) the primary-constituents have lost their foothold and like rocks fallen from the edge of a mountain incline towards dissolution, that is, full resorption into the transcendental core of the universe;
(7) the Self abides in its essential nature, undefiled and alone (*kevalin*).

The first four are referred to as the fourfold release (*vimukti*) pertaining to gnostic illumination, whereas the latter three are said to be the triple release of consciousness itself.

Patañjali, unfortunately, does not explain what he means by the phrase 'sevenfold transcendental-insight', presumably because it stands for a yogic theme well known to his contemporaries. We must, at any rate, be cautious towards Vyāsa's interpretation which may or may not be based on authentic information from within the tradition of Classical Yoga.

The Eightfold Yoga

Note: Now commences what must be regarded as a self-contained unit, either of the nature of a later interpolation or a lengthy quotation introduced by Patañjali himself because it contained a number of convenient definitions. Contrary to the opinion of most previous researchers who have dissected the *Yoga-Sūtra* into four and more 'texts', I consider this to be the only alien material in Patañjali's work. However, although we can be certain that II.28 constitutes the beginning of this insertion, textual analysis has failed to determine its exact ending, but in all likelihood Patañjali's text is resumed at III.9, if not already at III.4.

II.28 *yoga-aṅga-anuṣṭhānād-aśuddhi-kṣaye jñāna-dīptir-ā-viveka-khyāteḥ*

yoga = (see I.1)
aṅga = member (see I.31)
anuṣṭhāna = performance (from *anu* + √*sthā* 'to stand')
aśuddhi = impurity (from *a* + √*śudh* 'to purify')
kṣaya = dwindling (from √*kṣi* 'to destroy')
jñāna = knowledge, here: gnosis (see I.8)
dīpti = brilliance, here: radiance (from √*dīp* 'to blaze')
ā = up to
viveka = discernment (see II.15)
khyāti = vision (see I.16)

Through the performance of the members of Yoga, and with the dwindling of impurity, [there comes about] the radiance of gnosis [which develops] up to the vision of discernment.

Systematisation of the techniques employed to achieve the yogic goal of Self-realisation long precedes Patañjali's codification of Yoga. Already in the *Maitrāyaṇīya-Upaniṣad* which must be placed in the first or second century BC, a schema involving six members is expounded. This is the so-called *ṣaḍ-aṅga-yoga* which does not list *yama*, *niyama* and *āsana* as separate items but introduces a new element, viz. *tarka*, placed between *dhāraṇā* and *samādhi*. Several variants of this type are known. The tradition of eight members is, in a way, an elaboration of these earlier representations. What is of practical importance here is the fact that however many *aṅgas* are included in a given series, they do not constitute stages. Elsewhere I have suggested that the eight factors of Patañjali's Yoga could usefully be arranged in a circle since it is by their combined power that the *yogin* propels himself forward along the path of internalisation.[13]

In his material condition man is, according to Yoga, in a state of impurity or defilement—morally, physically and mentally, but above all from a metaphysical point of view. Through unwavering practice and the correct application of the techniques of Yoga, the *yogin* is able to transmute himself. Self-realisation is gained gradually, as the false projections and delusions are progressively retracted. This process has universally been symbolised as one of purification, baptism by fire. The radiance of gnosis occurs, and increases in intensity, when the ordinary consciousness is calmed and transformed (into the enstatic consciousness)—ending in the supreme realisation of the Self. The phrase 'up to the vision of discernment' appears to be a deliberate attempt to link the *aṣṭa-aṅga* material to the main body of the text; evidently it refers back to II.26.

II.29 *yama-niyama-āsana-prāṇāyāma-pratyāhāra-dhāraṇā-dhyāna-samādhayo' ṣṭāv-aṅgāni*

yama = restraint (from √*yam* 'to restrain')
niyama = observance (from *ni* + √*yam* 'to restrain')
āsana = posture (from √*ās* 'to sit')
prāṇāyāma = breath-control (from *prāṇa* + *ā* + √*yam* 'to restrain')
pratyāhāra = sense-withdrawal (from *prati* + *ā* + √*hṛ* 'to hold')
dhāraṇā = concentration (from √*dhṛ* 'to hold')
dhyāna = meditative-absorption (see I.39)
samādhi = enstasy (see I.20)
aṣṭa = eight

[13] See G. Feuerstein (1974[a]), p. 72.

aṅga = member (see I.31)

Restraint, observance, posture, breath-control, sense-withdrawal, concentration, meditative-absorption and enstasy are the eight members [of Yoga].

G. M. Koelman (1970) groups these eight components into four levels: (1) the somatic, (2) the ethical, (3) the psychical and (4) the metaphysical level. However, it is obvious that not all practices fit neatly into one particular category, and we must concede that they may partake of several levels. Thus, for instance, the practice of purification (*śauca*) as one of the items of observance (*niyama*) may comprise a physical cleansing process, a psychic process of catharsis and also a moral act of pure intention. In a sense, even the technique of meditative-absorption can be said to have ethical implications, which becomes particularly apparent with the exercise of projecting friendliness, compassion, etc. (see I.33). Man is a moral being and cannot escape the ethical consequences of his behaviour even if that be pure dedication to Self-realisation. Similarly, the practices of posture and breath-control are not exclusively bodily acts. They have also a psychic correlate, although among contemporary western students of Yoga this fact is all too often ignored, to the detriment of their own practice and well-being. By 'metaphysical level', Koelman means Self-realisation. Strictly speaking, this transcends the realm of yogic exertion as it transcends the entire orbit of cosmic existence.

II.30 *ahiṃsā-satya-asteya-brahmacarya-aparigrahā yamāḥ*

ahiṃsā = non-harming (from *a* + √*han* 'to hurt')
satya = truth, here: truthfulness (from √*as* 'to be')
asteya = non-stealing (from *a* + √*stā* 'to steal')
brahmacarya = lit. 'conduct of *brahma*', here: chastity (from *brahma* + √*car* 'to move')
aparigraha = greedlessness (from *a* + *pari* + √*grah* 'to grasp')
yama = restraint (see II.29)

Non-harming, truthfulness, non-stealing, chastity and greedlessness are the restraints.

The subjugation of one's appetites and the regulation and harmonisation of one's social relationships are essential prerequisites of Yoga. They are not only first steps on the path but form the very foundation of the whole yogic enterprise. At first the practice of these moral principles requires conscious effort, but as the *yogin*'s inner being becomes more attuned to the higher realities, the application of non-harming, truthfulness and the other virtues becomes habitual. Intentional stealing (and greed is a form of theft!), harming and deceit become virtually impossible for the accomplished *yogin*. Nor will the adept need to wrestle with his sexual drive any longer, or the neurotic phantasies resulting from forced abstention. For a more detailed explanation of the individual components of *yama*, I refer the reader to my *The Essence of Yoga* (pp. 75ff.).

II.31. *jāti-deśa-kāla-samaya-anavacchinnāḥ sarva-bhaumā mahā-vratam*

jāti = birth (see II.13)
deśa = place (from √*diś* 'to point out')
kāla = time (see I.14)
samaya = lit. 'coming together', here: circumstance (from *sam* + √*i* 'to go')
anavacchinna = lit. 'unseparated', here: irrespective of (from *an* + *ava* + √*chid* 'to cut')
sarva = all
bhauma = belonging to level, here: in (all) spheres
mahant = great
vrata = vow (from √*vṛ* 'to will')

[These are valid] in all spheres, irrespective of birth, place, time and circumstance [and constitute] the great vow.

Patañjali's ethical code is substantially identical with the moral principles advocated by the major religions of the world. Spirituality is not a disembodied, bloodless, abstract principle, but an activity 'in the flesh', involving real persons and concrete situations. No path to Self-realisation can circumvent the moral life of man. According to the *Yoga-Sūtra*, the five kinds of restraint or moral obligations are unconditionally valid. And this applies to the *yogin* as much as to the man of the world. Even though the *yogin*'s action is said to be neither black nor white (see IV.7)—this does not mean he is given *carte-blanche* to commit immoral acts. Rather his involutionary struggle is to be understood as an *a-moral* process.

II.32 *śauca-saṃtoṣa-tapaḥ-svādhyāya-īśvara-praṇidhānāni niyamāḥ*

śauca = purity (from √*śuc* 'to be radiant')

saṃtoṣa = contentment (from *sam* + √*tuṣ* 'to be satisfied')
tapas = ascesis, here: austerity (see II.1)
svādhyāya = self-study (see II.1)
īśvara = lord (see I.23)
praṇidhāna = devotion (see I.23)
niyama = observance (see II.29)

Purity, contentment, austerity, self-study and devotion to the Lord are the observances.

In contrast to the five types of restraint which are chiefly intended to regulate the *yogin*'s social life, the five observances are more concerned with self-discipline. Self-study or the dedicated entering into the spirit of the sacred lore and devotion to the Lord are already known to us from aphorism II.1. So is the practice of *tapas* which, in the present context, has evidently a more limited connotation than the *tapas* mentioned in Patañjali's text proper. I have therefore translated the term as 'austerity'. Purification, as Vyāsa informs us, comprises both physical and mental acts, and contentment is, in Vācaspati Miśra's words, 'the desire for no more than is necessary for the maintenance of life'.

II.33 *vitarka-bādhane pratipakṣa-bhāvanam*

vitarka = cogitation, here: unwholesome-deliberation (see I.17)
bādhana = repelling (from √*bādh* 'to repel')
pratipakṣa = opposite (from *prati* + *pakṣa* 'side, wing')
bhāvana = cultivation (see I.28)

For the repelling of unwholesome-deliberation [the *yogin* should pursue] the cultivation of the opposite.

Vitarka is here manifestly used in a different sense from that of aphorism I.17 where it stands for a specific act of consciousness in the enstatic state. In the present context it represents a rather more mundane mental event, namely that kind of deliberation which contravenes the moral code of Yoga. More precisely, it denotes such unwholesome thoughts, wishes or intentions as hurting others, stealing from others and similar failings. When such ideas occur, rather than rationalising them away, perhaps by bending the moral principles, the *yogin* is enjoined to recall their opposites, that is, their moral counterparts. Very probably *bhāvana* entails more than the mere rational act of reminding oneself of the wholesome principle which one is about to infringe. Depending on the seriousness of one's immoral intentions, it could possibly be extended into a full-fledged meditational exercise. Also, the idea of 'cultivation' implies a continuous effort and the possibility of gradual moral improvement.

II.34 *vitarkā hiṃsā-ādayaḥ kṛta-kārita-anumoditā lobha-krodha-moha-pūrvakā mṛdu-madhya-adhimātrā duḥkha-ajñāna-ananta-phalā iti pratipakṣa-bhāvanam*

vitarka = cogitation, here: unwholesome-deliberation (see I.17)
hiṃsā = harming (see II.30)
ādi = *et cetera*
kṛta = done (from √*kṛ* 'to do')
kārita = caused to be done (from √*kṛ* 'to do')
anumodita = approved (from *anu* + √*mud* 'to rejoice')
lobha = greed (from √*lubh* 'to desire')
krodha = anger (from √*krudh* 'to be angry')
moha = infatuation (from √*muh* 'to be deluded')
pūrvaka = preceding, here: arising from
mṛdu = modest (see I.22)
madhya = medium (see I.22)
adhimātra = excessive (see I.22)
duḥkha = sorrow (see I.31)
ajñāna = nescience (see I.8)
ananta = unending (see II.47)
phala = fruit, here: fruition (see II.14)
iti = thus
pratipakṣa = opposite (see II.33)
bhāvana = cultivation (see I.28)

The unwholesome-deliberations, [such as] harming *et cetera*, [whether] done, caused to be done or approved, [whether] arising from greed, anger or infatuation, [whether] modest, medium or excessive—[these find their] unending fruition in nescience and sorrow; thus [the *yogin* should devote himself to] the cultivation of [their] opposites.

This aphorism leaves no trace of doubt about the strictness with which all unwholesome impulses are expected to be repelled. Whatever their reason and however mild they may be, they are bound to lead the *yogin* astray and intensify his spiritual blindness and enhance his profound dissatisfaction with mundane life. Only the steadfast adherence to the principles of Yoga can prevent a slipping back into the natural attitude for which intentional harming (e.g. warfare, competition), stealing (e.g. tax evasion) or lying (e.g. advertising) seem justifiable.

II.35 *ahiṃsā-pratiṣṭhāyāṃ tat-saṃnidhau vaira-tyāgaḥ*

ahiṃsā = non-harming (see II.30)
pratiṣṭhāya = being grounded in (from *pra* + √*sthā* 'to stand')
tad = that, here: his
saṃnidhi = proximity, here: presence (from *sam* + *ni* + √*dhā* 'to put')
vaira = enmity (from √*vī* 'to fall upon')
tyāga = abandonment, here: abandoned (from √*tyaj* 'to abandon')

When [the *yogin*] is grounded in [the virtue] of non-harming, [all] enmity is abandoned in his presence.

Self-realisation is by definition a happening beyond the ken of the normal space-time world, and the path to it presupposes the all-out negation of everything worldly (in consciousness). This has given rise to the accusation that Yoga is basically an egotistic, narcissistic concern, which leaves the world as it is without regard for one's fellow men. That this opinion is misguided can be seen from the present *sūtra*. The transformation of the *yogin*'s private universe remains not without wholesome repercussions in his environment. True, the *yogin* may not bequeath to his society magnificent works of art or great scientific inventions, but neither does he exacerbate the plight of his contemporaries by competing with them for power, status, honour or wealth. On the contrary, his total centredness and psychic self-sufficiency make him a resting-point, a haven of peace, for those who seek respite from the hustle of everyday existence. There is no dearth of popular stories, some no doubt partly true, of *yogins* who by their sheer presence are able to transform their immediate surroundings and to communicate to others some of their inner peace and tranquillity and occasionally to implant in receptive minds a spark of the lucidity of which they partake.

Non-harming, when cultivated to perfection, is an attitude, a state of being, which transmits itself to others to the extent that all feelings of antagonism cease in the presence of the *yogin*. It is tempting to ask whether this undesigned harmonising influence is not as positive a contribution to human civilisation as any scientific discovery, and with the additional advantage of no negative side-effects whatsoever.

II.36 *satya-pratiṣṭhāyāṃ kriyā-phala-āśrayatvam*
satya = truthfulness (see II.30)
pratiṣṭhāya = being grounded in (see II.34)
kriyā = action (see II.1)
phala = fruit, here: fruition (see II.14)
āśrayatva = dependency, here: depend (from *ā* + √*śri* 'to rest on')
When grounded in truthfulness, action [and its] fruition depend [on him].

Vyāsa interprets this aphorism as declaring that whatever the adept predicts comes true, or else he would not commit himself. One must not push this claim too far. Significantly, Vyāsa confines himself to examples which concern spiritual matters, e.g. when the *yogin* enjoins a follower to live a morally sound life his injunction will not be in vain. In the Purāṇas, which are folkloristic compilations, we meet with yogic heroes who, by dint of their enormous will-power, can cause the sun to stop still or perform similar miraculous feats. Such stories are, of course, entirely allegorical and have a didactic purpose.

II.37 *asteya-pratiṣṭhāyāṃ sarva-ratna-upasthānam*
asteya = non-stealing (see II.30)
pratiṣṭhāya = being grounded in (see II.34)
sarva = all
ratna = jewel (from √*rā* 'to bestow')
upasthāna = approach, here: appear (from *upa* + √*sthā* 'to stand')
When grounded in non-stealing, all [kinds of] jewels appear [for him].

Literally interpreted this aphorism makes little sense. As I. K. Taimni remarked, it 'does not mean that precious stones begin to fly through the air and fall at his feet. It is a way of saying that he becomes aware of all kinds of treasures in his vicinity.'[14] Possibly even this interpretation is too materialistic.

II.38 *brahmacarya-pratiṣṭhāyāṃ vīrya-lābhaḥ*
brahmacarya = chastity (see II.30)
pratiṣṭhāya = being grounded in (see II.34)
vīrya = vigour, vitality (see II.34 *vaira*)

[14] I. K. Taimni (1961), p. 241.

lābha = obtainment, here: acquired (from √*labh* 'to obtain')
When grounded in chastity, [great] vitality is acquired.

The conservation of sexual energy is an important aspect of yogic practice. Long before Sigmund Freud shocked Viennese society with the discovery that *homo sapiens* is also (or, as he saw it, is primarily) a sexual being, the *yogins* of India had acknowledged and harnessed the powerful, undirected sexual drive in man. In popular thinking the *yogin* became the ascetic whose semen flows upwards (*ūrdhva-retas*), that is, whose sexual energy is continually transmuted ('sublimated'). Chastity, which is to be practised in thought and deed, rather than turning the *yogin* into an impotent weakling, greatly increases his vitality. Considering the extraordinary concentration of effort demanded of him, such vigour is indeed imperative.

II.39 *aparigraha-sthairye janma-kathaṃtā-saṃbodhaḥ*
aparigraha = greedlessness (see II.30)
sthairya = being settled, here: steadied (from √*sthā* 'to stand')
janman = birth (see II.12)
kathaṃtā = lit. 'why-ness', here: the wherefore (from *katha*)
saṃbodha = knowledge (from *sam* + √*budh* 'to know')
When steadied in greedlessness [he secures] knowledge of the wherefore of [his] birth(s).

Greedlessness, which is the renunciation of the desire for possessions, is the correlative of the gradual suspension of the ego identity in favour of the transcendental Self. This progressive identity shift gives man access to the depth-memory which not only acts as the reservoir of the subliminal-activators generated in his present embodiment but also contains the traits (*vāsanā*) stored from the distilled life-experience of former births.

II..40 *śaucāt-sva-aṅga-jugupsā parair-asaṃsargaḥ*
śauca = purity (see II.32)
sva = own
aṅga = member, here: limb (see I.31)
jugupsā = disgust, here: distance (from √*gup* 'to protect')
para = other

asaṃsarga = non-association, here: non-contamination (from *a* + *sam* + √*sṛj* 'to emit')

Through purity [he gains] distance towards his own limbs [and also] [the desire for] non-contamination by others.

Commonly translated with 'disgust', the interesting term *jugupsā* really conveys a more positive idea, namely that of being on one's guard with respect to the body, of having a detached attitude towards our mortal frame. At the same time, however, the *yogin* is concerned that there should not be renewed contamination (i.e. distraction!) by others, and he accordingly opts for a solitary life in the forest or high up in the mountains. This may seem like vapid snobbery on his part, but the *yogin*'s attitude is not one of scorn or disparagement, merely one of wariness. As long as he has not attained perfect self-control, he understandably does not wish to run even the slightest risk of being diverted from his anyhow difficult and precarious project.

II.41 *sattva-śuddhi-saumanasya-eka-agrya-indriya-jaya-ātma-darśana-yogyatvāni ca*

sattva = lit. 'being-ness', here: left untranslated (from √*as* 'to be')
śuddhi = purity (see II.28)
saumanasya = gladness (from *su* + √*man* 'to think' + *as* + *ya*)
eka = one } here: one-pointedness
agrya = pointed(ness) }
indriya = sense-organ (see II.18)
jaya = mastery (from √*ji* 'to win')
ātman = self (see II.5)
darśana = vision (see I.30)
yogyatva = fitness, here: capability (see II.53 *yogyatā*)
ca = and

[Furthermore:] purity of *sattva*, gladness, one-pointedness, mastery of the sense-organs and the capability for self-vision [are achieved].

The cultivation of purity has important consequences. It leads to the purity of one's inner being. The term *sattva* has a number of connotations which cannot all be captured in a single English word. I have therefore left it untranslated. *Sattva*, among other things, is the lucidity factor of consciousness, that is, its highest form of manifestation. In fact, one way of characterising the yogic process is in terms of a gradual replacement of the *rajas* and *tamas* factors by *sattva*. On the emotional level this induces a sustained feeling of gladness, joy. Attention becomes intensified, 'one-pointed', and the adept acquires the ability to exclude all sensory input from his surroundings.

II.42 *saṃtosād-anuttamaḥ sukha-lābhaḥ*

saṃtoṣa = contentment (see II.32)
anuttama = unexcelled (from *an* + *ud* + *tama*)
sukha = joy (see I.33)
lābha = obtainment, here: gained (see II.38)

Through contentment unexcelled joy is gained.

Vyāsa quotes a popular saying from the *Mahābhārata* (XII.174.46) to illustrate what is meant: 'What is [regarded as] sensual pleasure in this world and what is [regarded as] celestial superb pleasure—these are not equal to a sixteenth part of the pleasure [which ensues after] the dwindling of the thirst [for life].'

II.43 *kāya-indriya-siddhir-aśuddhi-kṣayāt-tapasaḥ*

kāya = body
indriya = sense-organ (see II.18)
siddhi = perfection (from √*sidh* 'to succeed')
aśuddhi = impurity (see II.28)
kṣaya = dwindling (see II.28)
tapas = austerity (see II.1)

Through austerity, on account of the dwindling of impurity, perfection of the body and the sense-organs [is gained].

The practice of *tapas* can consist of such diverse exercises as fasting, standing or sitting stock-still, observing complete silence, or voluntarily exposing oneself to heat, cold, hunger and thirst, etc. The *Mahābhārata* and the purāṇic literature know of numerous ascetics who mortify their flesh in this way. What is meant by perfection of the body is explained in III.45.

II.44 *svādhyāyād-iṣṭa-devatā-saṃprayogaḥ*

svādhyāya = self-study (see II.1)
iṣṭa = desired, chosen (from √*iṣ* 'to desire')
devatā = deity (from √*div* 'to shine')

saṃprayoga = contact (from *sam* + *pra* + √*yuj* 'to join')
Through self-study [the *yogin* establishes] contact with the chosen deity.

Self-study, as we have seen, means the recitation, silent or aloud, and subsequent meditation of the sacred lore. This practice is taken from the liturgy of the hindu priests. The holy texts, especially the Vedas, are thought to be supercharged with a numinous power, each word (*mantra*) being a vehicle of that power. Therefore, the scriptures must be used, that is, pronounced and intoned, with the utmost circumspection. Meticulous recitation centralises one's attention and thus internalises consciousness. This insight has been converted into a whole philosophy and technology by the masters of the tantric schools. Associated with the practice of *mantra* recitation is the likewise popular notion of deities (*devatā*), real or imaginary, which are essentially connected with certain scriptures, rituals and other objects or tasks. These are the gods depicted in iconography.

Through self-study or the intellectual penetration into the deeper levels of significance of a selected scripture and its presiding deity, the *yogin* makes contact with that god or goddess. This occurs in the form of a meditational experience. It is noteworthy that in buddhist Tantrism where these deities are explicitly denied any objective existence, this visionary encounter is always described as an acutely realistic experience. At any rate, it is obvious that this must not be misconstrued to mean a union with *īśvara*. Such a notion is foreign to Classical Yoga.

II.45 *samādhi-siddhir-īśvara-praṇidhānāt*
samādhi = enstasy (see I.20)
siddhi = perfection, here: attainment (see II.43)
īśvara = lord (see I.23)
praṇidhāna = devotion (see I.23)
Through devotion to the Lord [comes about] the attainment of enstasy.

The decisive word here is *siddhi* which can mean either 'perfection' or 'attainment'. Whichever meaning is intended by Patañjali, this aphorism clearly underscores the signal importance of *īśvara* in Yoga. It is not evident whether *siddhi*, in either of the two senses, should be understood as a sufficient and necessary condition or as a sufficient condition. In other words, is *īśvara-praṇidhāna* the only means to perfect or attain the enstatic consciousness? Or is it merely one of several ways of achieving the same transformation of consciousness? Vācaspati Miśra stresses the centrality of devotion to the Lord, stating that the other seven techniques (i.e. the members or *aṅga*) are merely subsidiary. Vyāsa (to III.6) even goes so far as to explain the *yogin*'s ability to move onto the next higher plane of enstasy as a direct result of the grace (*prasāda*) of the Lord. Implicit in these contentions is the interpretation of the term *siddhi* in the more radical sense of 'attainment'. On the other hand, 'perfection' of enstasy could meaningfully refer to the attainment of the higher forms of enstatic consciousness (such as *asaṃprajñāta-samādhi*), but this presupposes that the lower types of enstasy may be brought about without devotion to the Lord. According to aphorism I.23, devotion to the Lord is a possible, not a necessary, aid to the realisation of enstasy. But then, we must remember that *īśvara-praṇidhāna* may well have a more central position within the framework of the *aṣṭa-aṅga* tradition than it appears to have in Kriyā-Yoga.

II.46 *sthira-sukham-āsanam*

sthira = steady (from √*sthā* 'to stand')
sukha = joy, here: comfortable (see I.33)
āsana = posture (see II.29)

The posture [should be] steady and comfortable.

Just as *mantra* recitation and visualisation exercises involving one's chosen deity have been massively elaborated in medieval Tantrism, so also has the yogic *āsana* inspired later masters of the Haṭhayoga school to evolve a whole system of postures. For Patañjali, however, *āsana* is exclusively a meditational aid. By contrast, the majority of postural exercises, developed in Haṭhayoga, serve an entirely different purpose, namely that of gaining mastery over the physiological processes. Even in the case of those postures which are meant as meditational seats, the physiological side-effects have been carefully noted in the scriptures. In Kriyā-Yoga, posture has to meet two basic requirements only; it must be suitable for immobilising the body and it must be comfortable so as not to interfere with the ongoing mental concentration. Vācaspati Miśra mentions the use of a yogic table (*yoga-paṭṭaka*) which is a kind of arm-rest invented to minimise muscular strain.

II.47 *prayatna-śaithilya-ananta-samāpattibhyām*

prayatna = effort, here: tension (from *pra* + √*yat* 'to endeavour')

śaithilya = relaxation (from *śithila* 'loose')
ananta = endless, here: the infinite (see II.34)
samāpatti = coincidence, here: coinciding (see I.41)

[It is accompanied] by the relaxation of tension and the coinciding with the infinite [consciousness-space].

All kinds of fanciful explanations have been proposed for this aphorism. But it seems to describe a simple psycho-physiological experience which can be verified by anyone who cares to cultivate posture properly. This is the sensation that the body—or rather one's image of it—'loosens up' and widens. It is unlikely that the word *ananta* refers to the mythological serpent-king Ananta, although symbolic overtones may be present; more probably, it is descriptive of the feeling of becoming extended beyond the skin characteristic of deep relaxation, and of merging with the surrounding infinite (consciousness) space.

II.48 *tato dvandva-anabhighātāḥ*

tatas = thence (see I.22)
dvandva = lit. 'two-two', pair, here: pair-of-opposites (from *dva* + *dva*)
anabhighāta = unassailability (from *an* + *abhi* + √*han* 'to strike')

Thence [results] unassailability by the pairs-of-opposites.

The pairs-of-opposites, such as heat–cold, humidity–aridity, pain–pleasure, etc., to which we are exposed in the ordinary waking consciousness *via* the sensory channels, are eliminated by the accomplishment of posture. This drives home the all-important point, usually overlooked by the western Yoga enthusiasts, that *āsana* is not *just* a physical exercise, but has a strong psychic component as well. Relaxed posture is the foundation of the practice of sense-withdrawal. When the body is perfectly relaxed, a pin prick and, at a more advanced stage, even the dentist's drill fail to cause the familiar sensation of pain.

II.49 *tasmin-sati śvāsa-praśvāsayor-gati-vicchedaḥ prāṇāyāmaḥ*

tasmin = in this (from *tad*) }
sati = being (see II.13) } here: when this is (achieved)
śvāsa = inhalation (from √*śvas* 'to breathe')
praśvāsa = exhalation (from *pra* + √*śvas* 'to breathe')
gati = course, here: flow (from √*gam* 'to go')

viccheda = cutting-off (see II.4)
prāṇāyāma = breath-control (from *prāṇa* + *āyāma*, see II.29)

When this is [achieved], breath-control [which is] the cutting-off of the flow of inhalation and exhalation [should be practised].

When posture is mastered, that is, when complete relaxation has set in, the practice of breath-control can commence, for the breath must be able to flow freely. Breath-control is not mere rhythmic breathing; its proper focus is on the pause between inhalation and exhalation. For, as Bhojarāja (to I.34) observed: 'The suppressed breath effects the one-pointedness of consciousness by means of the restriction of all sense activity.' Thus there is a direct correspondence between *stambha-vṛtti* (the fixed phase of breathing) and the restriction of the fluctuations of consciousness.

II.50 *bāhya-abhyantara-stambha-vṛttir-deśa-kāla-saṃkhyābhiḥ paridṛṣṭo dīrgha-sūkṣmaḥ*

bāhya = external (from √*bah* 'to increase')
abhyantara = internal (from *abhi* + *antara*)
stambha = fixed (from √*stambh* 'to stop')
vṛtti = fluctuation, here: movement (see I.2)
deśa = place (see II.31)
kāla = time (see I.14)
saṃkhyā = number (from *sam* + √*khyā* 'to be mentioned')
paridṛṣṭa = lit. 'viewed', here: regulated (from *pari* + √*dṛś* 'to see')
dīrgha = protracted (see I.14)
sūkṣma = subtle, here: contracted (see I.44)

[Breath-control is] external, internal and fixed in its movement, [and it is] regulated by place, time and number; [it can be] protracted or contracted.

Breath-control comprises three phases, viz. expiration, inspiration and retention. 'Place', according to Vyāsa, does not refer to the environment in which *prāṇāyāma* should be practised, but to the location within the body where the breath (or vital force) is to be directed, e.g. the space between navel and palate, etc. 'Time' denotes the length of the inspirations and expirations, while 'number' stands for the number of repetitions. A further factor is the intensity with which the breath is expelled and drawn in.

II.51 *bāhya-abhyantara-viṣaya-ākṣepī caturthaḥ*
bāhya = external (see II.50)
abhyantara = internal (see II.50)
viṣaya = object, here: sphere (see I.11)
ākṣepin = transcending (from *ā* = √*kṣip* 'to cast')
caturtha = fourth (from *catur* 'four')
[The movement of breath] transcending the external and internal sphere is the 'fourth'.

This generally misunderstood aphorism could possibly be a reference to a special phenomenon occurring in the enstatic state, where breathing can become so reduced and shallow that it cannot be detected by unaided observation. This state of suspended breathing can continue for considerable periods which, in normal circumstances, would indicate certain death. This fourth mode of breathing is thus, properly speaking, not a form of voluntary breath-control at all, but is simply the physiological correlate of an extraordinary state of consciousness.

II.52 *tataḥ kṣīyate prakāśa-āvaraṇam*
tatas = thence (see I.22)
kṣīyate = disappears (from √*kṣi* 'to decrease'; one of the few verbs found in the text)
prakāśa = light (from *pra* + √*kāś* 'to shine')
āvaraṇa = covering (from *ā* + √*vṛ* 'to cover')
Thence the covering of the [inner] light disappears.

This aphorism belongs to II.49–50 rather than II.51 (which is best regarded as an after-thought explaining a unique type of breath restraint). Breath-control interiorises the consciousness further, inducing a peculiar condition of inner luminosity which, in turn, facilitates concentration as is explained in the next *sūtra*.

II.53 *dhāraṇāsu ca yogyatā manasaḥ*
dhāraṇā = concentration (see II.29)
ca = and
yogyatā = fitness (see II.41 *yogyatva*)
manas = mind (see I.35)
And [the *yogin* gains] the fitness of the mind for concentration.

This aphorism invites comparison with *sūtra* I.34, where Patañjali declares that the restriction of the whirlpools of the mind can also be stilled by the controlled expulsion and retention of the breath.

II.54 *sva-viṣaya-asaṃprayoge cittasya sva-rūpa-anukāra iva-indriyāṇāṃ pratyāhāraḥ*

sva = own, here: their
viṣaya = object (see I.11)
asaṃprayoga = disunion, here: disuniting (from *a* + *sam* + *pra* + √*yuj* 'to join')
citta = consciousness (see I.2)
sva = own
rūpa = form
anukāra = imitation (from *anu* + √*kṛ* 'to do')
iva = as it were
indriya = sense-organ (see II.18)
pratyāhāra = sense-withdrawal (see II.29)

Sense-withdrawal is the imitation as it were of the own-form of consciousness [on the part] of the sense-organs by disuniting [themselves] from their objects.

Vyāsa illustrates this succinct definition by a vivid metaphor: 'As when the queen-bee flies up and the bees swarm after her and when she settles down [they also] settle, so the senses are restricted when consciousness is restricted.' Sensory inhibition and the restriction of consciousness activity are obverse and reverse of the same basic process. So long as there is sensory input, consciousness is not at rest. However, when attention is focused on an internal object sensory activity is at first partially, then totally eliminated.

II.55 *tataḥ paramā vaśyatā-indriyāṇām*

tatas = thence (see I.22)
parama = supreme (from *para*)
vaśyatā = subjugation, here: obedience (from √*vaś* 'to will' + *ya* + *tā*)
indriya = sense-organ (see II.18)

Thence [results] the supreme obedience of the sense-organs.

At the highest stage of accomplishment in sense-withdrawal, the *yogin* can block out individual sensory inputs at will, or even inhibit all sense activity at once. The image of obedience can be explained from a passage in the *Kaṭha Upaniṣad*, one of the earliest texts of this genre which deals with Yoga: 'Know the Self as the chariot-master, the body as the chariot; know the wisdom-faculty (*buddhi*) as the charioteer and the mind as the reins. The senses, they say, are the horses and the sense-objects are [their] arena . . . (III.3–4[a]).'

Practising the Royal Yoga and having attained the state [which yields such powers as] miniaturisation *et cetera*, [the *yogin*] becomes resplendent.
Yogaśikhā-Upaniṣad I.138[a]

Chapter Three
VIBHŪTI-PĀDA

The accomplishments
The superpowers (what you can develop

Note: According to traditional explanations, the third *pāda* deals, as its title indicates, with the so-called supernormal powers or *vibhūtis*. The word *vibhūti*, significantly enough, appears nowhere in the text itself. These extraordinary powers, ascribed to the accomplished *yogin*, are said to be the product of constraint (*saṃyama*) which is the practice of concentration, meditative-absorption and enstasy in regard to the same object. However, there is a good deal of other material in the third chapter which is perhaps of even greater significance than the treatment of the supernormal powers. It is possible that *vibhūti*, instead of referring exclusively to these magical achievements, has a wider meaning. Etymologically, the word is derived from the prefix *vi*, the verbal root √*bhū* 'to become' and the suffix *ti*, and it has the literal meaning of 'that which extends far'. In this more general sense it could well denote also the enstatic condition.

III.1 *deśa-bandhaś-cittasya dhāraṇā*

deśa = place, here: spot (see II.31)
bandha = binding (from √*bandh* 'to bind')
citta = consciousness (see I.2)
dhāraṇā = concentration (see II.29)

Concentration is the binding of consciousness to a [single] spot.

Like sense-withdrawal and the other *aṅgas,* concentration constitutes a particular *technique* of Yoga and must not be reduced to mean attention in general. As coinciding (*samāpatti*) is the underlying *process* of the technique of enstasy so one-pointedness (*eka-agratā*) is the underlying process of the technique of concentration. This focusing of the mind is what is meant by the binding of consciousness. Place, as we learn from the commentaries, signifies either an internal or an external object. However, Vācaspati Miśra is mistaken when he identifies concentration on an external object with the practice of *traṭāka* or gazing which is widely employed in Haṭhayoga. In *traṭāka* the eyes are kept open and the sight is fixed on an object actually extraneous to consciousness, thus involving an act of perception. Yet, it is clear from the *Yoga-Sūtra* that concentration follows upon sense-withdrawal or is coterminous with it. External object (*bāhya-viṣaya*) can therefore only mean an internalised external object, that is, the image or idea of a real object. Internal object (*antara-viṣaya*), on the other hand, denotes the various places within the body (e.g. navel, heart, etc.) which are the favourite anchorages for consciousness mentioned in Yoga texts.

III.2 *tatra pratyaya-ekatānatā dhyānam*

tatra = therein, here: with regard to that (see I.13)
pratyaya = presented-idea (see I.10)
eka = one } here: one-directionality
tānatā = lit. 'extension' (from √*tan* 'to stretch' + *tā*) } here: one-directionality
dhyāna = meditative-absorption (see I.39)

The one-directionality of the presented-ideas with regard to that [object of concentration] is meditative-absorption.

Sense-withdrawal, concentration and meditative-absorption are continuous and part of the same process of interiorisation. *Dhyāna* is that particular phase of yogic introversion in which the presented-ideas are consistently associated with the object of concentration until no foreign thoughts intrude and complete restriction (*nirodha*) is achieved.

III.3 *tad-eva-artha-mātra-nirbhāsaṃ sva-rūpa-śūnya-iva samādiḥ*

tad = that
eva = verily, here: left untranslated
artha = purpose, here: object (see I.28)
mātra = only
nirbhāsa = shining forth (see I.43)

sva = own } here: essence
rūpa = form }
śūnya = empty (see I.9)
iva = as it were, here: as if
samādhi = enstasy (see I.20)

That [consciousness], [when] shining forth as the object only as if empty of [its] essence, is enstasy.

Vyāsa and Vācaspati Miśra understand this highly technical aphorism differently. Their reading is as follows: When meditative-absorption shines forth in the form of the intended object only, in other words, when it is fused with it, it has in a way lost its own characteristic mode of functioning which is the splitting up of subject and object. However, since meditative-absorption is strictly speaking a technique and not the special type of consciousness induced by it, the initial word *tad* must be taken to refer to the one-directed flow of presented-ideas mentioned in III.2, that is, the fully absorbed consciousness.

III.4 *trayam-ekatra saṃyamaḥ*

traya = triple, here: the three (from *tri* 'three')
ekatra = in one, here: together (from *eka* 'one')
saṃyama = constraint (from *sam* + √*yam* 'to restrain')

The three [practised] together [on the same object] are constraint.

The practice of concentration, meditative-absorption and enstasy with respect to one and the same object is technically known as constraint.

III.5 *taj-jayāt prajñā-ālokaḥ*

tad = that
jaya = conquest, here: mastery (see II.41)
prajñā = transcendental-insight (see I.20)
āloka = flashing-forth (from *ā* + √*lok* 'to perceive')

Through mastery of that [practice of constraint] [there ensues] the flashing-forth of transcendental-insight.

Constraint (*saṃyama*) proceeds by stages, and as the *yogin* reaches the full depth of the enstatic experience, i.e. *nirvicāra-samādhi*, consciousness becomes motionless, transparent. In this state of utter lucidity the shift from the conscious self to the transcendental

Self occurs. Provided that this interpretation is correct, *prajñā-āloka* may be considered as a synonym of *viveka-khyāti*, the vision of discernment (see II.28).

III.6 *tasya bhūmiṣu viniyogaḥ*

tasya = of it, here: its
bhūmi = stage, here: gradual (see I.14).
viniyoga = application, here: progression (from *vi* + *ni* + √*yuj* 'to yoke')

Its progression is gradual.

Constraint is not all of a piece, but comprises, as we have seen (see I.17, I.42–4), several stages. However, this schema serves only as a general model, and in actual practice progression can vary. This seems to be the point which Vyāsa is trying to make when he remarks that 'Yoga itself is the teacher' (*yoga eva-upādhyāyaḥ*); he adds the following well-known quotation from an unknown source:

By Yoga, Yoga must be known;
Through Yoga, Yoga advances;
He who cares for Yoga,
In Yoga rests forever.

III.7 *trayam-antar-aṅgaṃ pūrvebhyaḥ*

traya = the three (see III.4)
antar = inner
aṅga = member (see I.31)
pūrva = previous

[In relation to] the previous [five techniques of Yoga] the three [components of constraint] are inner members.

Restraint, observance, posture, breath-control and sense-withdrawal are designated as the outer members (*bahir-aṅga*) of the body of Yoga, for the patent reason that they regulate the external relations of the *yogin*. By the same token, concentration, meditative-absorption and enstasy are considered as inner members since their appropriate sphere of action is consciousness itself.

III.8 *tad-api bahir-aṅgaṃ nirbījasya*

tad = that, here: they
api = also, here: yet
bahis = outer

aṅga = member (see I.31)
nirbīja = seedless (from *nir* + *bīja* 'seed')

Yet they are outer members [in relation to] the seedless [enstasy].

By comparison with the highest form of ultra-cognitive *samādhi* (see I.51), the combined practices of concentration, meditative-absorption and enstasy (in the sense of *saṃprajñāta-samādhi*), are merely external aids. The seedless enstasy represents the climax of the process of interiorisation.

Note: Very probably the next aphorism belongs to Patañjali's own text again.

III.9 *vyutthāna-nirodha-saṃskārayor-abhibhava-prādur-bhāvau nirodha-kṣaṇa-citta-anvayo nirodha-pariṇāmaḥ*

vyutthāna = emergence (from *vi* + *ud* + √*sthā* 'to stand')
nirodha = restriction (see I.2)
saṃskāra = subliminal-activator (see I.18)
abhibhava = subjugation (from *abhi* + √*bhū* 'to become')
prādur = lit. 'outdoor' (from *pra* + *dur* 'door') } here: manifestation
bhāva = becoming (from √*bhū* 'to become') }
nirodha = restriction (see I.2)
kṣaṇa = moment (from √*kṣan* 'to break')
citta = consciousness
anvaya = nexus, here: connected with (from *anu* + √*i* 'to go')
nirodha = restriction (see I.2)
pariṇāma = transformation (see II.15)

[When there is] subjugation of the subliminal-activators of emergence and the manifestation of the subliminal-activators of restriction—[this is] the restriction transformation which is connected with consciousness [in its] moment of restriction.

The group of aphorisms III.9–15 deal with rather recondite aspects of Yoga theory. The key term of this particular passage is *pariṇāma* or 'transformation'. The apparent purpose of these *sūtras* is to restate the dynamics of the gradual transmutation of the waking consciousness into the enstatic consciousness in terms of the specific theory of causation subscribed to by Patañjali.

The *pariṇāma* concept has been elaborated in answer to the searching question as to how change is at all possible. The Self is by definition unchanging transcendental awareness, but Nature *is* incessant change. Yoga, like Sāṃkhya, denies that the changes we observe are unreal, as is the contention of the Vedānta philosophers. More than that, the states or conditions of change have a real base, namely *prakṛti*, for something cannot emerge from nothing. Transformation, therefore, means the disappearance of one real condition (*avasthā*) and the appearance of another equally real condition of the same substratum. Put differently (see III.14), *prakṛti* is the permanent 'substance' (*dharmin*) and its series of manifestations are the 'qualities' (*dharma*).

How does this apply to the present aphorism? Here consciousness is looked upon as the 'substance' which remains constant throughout the changes that occur by means of the practices of Yoga, especially the technique of constraint. Again, the subliminal-activators and presented-ideas are considered as 'aspects' (*dharma*) of that single, constant substance. Hence consciousness is by no means eliminated when the presented-ideas alone are inhibited; the other aspect of consciousness, viz. the matrix of subliminal-activators must likewise be destroyed. The present aphorism translates the restriction spoken of in I.2 into the philosophical language of 'change'. Thus the condition of restriction is due to the actualisation of a distinct kind of subliminal-activators inhibiting those subliminal-activators which cause consciousness to turn outward. However, those inhibited subliminal-activators are not destroyed; they simply become latent. For *prakṛti* cannot be destroyed. Destruction is merely apparent destruction inasmuch as it is relative to the experiencing consciousness. Nor is the creation of subliminal-activators, favourable to the condition of restriction, a proper creation; more precisely, it is the actualisation of ever-present possibilities within Nature. The state of restriction is thought to be composed of momentary (*kṣaṇa*) impulses towards restriction. In fact, all states of consciousness consist in such series of moments (*kṣaṇa*), since time itself is a succession (*krama*) of structural units.

III.10 *tasya praśānta-vāhitā saṃskārāt*

tasya = of this
praśānta = calm (from *pra* + √*śam* 'to be calm')
vāhitā = flow (from √*vah* 'to bear along')
saṃskāra = subliminal-activator (see I.18)

The calm flow of this [consciousness] [is effected] through subliminal-activators.

The 'calm flow' is a specific transformation of consciousness brought about by a succession of subliminal-activators tending towards the inhibition of the subliminal-activators of emergence. Judging from the following two aphorisms, the expression 'calm flow' is descriptive of meditative-absorption in particular.

III.11 *sarva-arthatā-ekāgratayoḥ kṣaya-udaya cittasya samādhi-pariṇāmaḥ*

sarva = all
arthatā = lit. 'object-ness' (see I.28)
ekāgratā = one-pointedness (see II.41 *ekāgrya*)
kṣaya = dwindling (see II.28)
udaya = uprising (from *ud* + √*i* 'to go')
citta = consciousness (see I.2)
samādhi = enstasy (see I.20)
pariṇāma = transformation (see II.15)

The dwindling of all-objectness and the uprising of one-pointedness is the enstasy transformation of consciousness.

The transformation of consciousness peculiar to enstasy is founded on the replacement of the cluster of objects (ideas) occupying the ordinary consciousness by one-pointedness, or the attention focused on a single spot. 'Dispersiveness', as J. H. Woods translates the compound *sarva-arthatā*, and 'one-pointedness' are two fundamental aspects (*dharma*) of consciousness. These two forms of manifestation can also be circumscribed by the terms centrifugality and centripetality. The task of the *yogin* lies in the gradual overcoming of the centrifugal tendency and the simultaneous cultivation of the centripetal tendency, that is, interiorisation.

III.12 *tataḥ punaḥ śānta-uditau tulya-pratyayau cittasya-ekāgratā-pariṇāmaḥ*

tatas = thence, here: then (see I.22)
punar = again
śānta = quiescent (see III.10)
udita = uprisen (from *ud* + √*i* 'to go')
tulya = similar (from √*tul* 'to compare with')
pratyaya = presented-idea (see I.10)
citta = consciousness (see I.2)
ekāgratā = one-pointedness (see III.11)
pariṇāma = transformation (see II.15)

Then again, when the quiescent and the uprisen presented-ideas are similar, [this is] the one-pointedness transformation of consciousness.

Just as the sudden shift from a consciousness space crowded with innumerable ideas to a consciousness which is one-pointed (in enstasy) can be explained in terms of a particular form of change, so also the one-pointedness in the enstatic state can be looked upon as a form of change. As Patañjali puts it, one-pointedness is composed of a succession of similar presented-ideas which flash up momentarily in consciousness.

III.13 *etena bhūta-indriyeṣu dharma-lakṣaṇa-avasthā-pariṇāmā vyākhyātāḥ*

etena = by this (from *etad* 'this')
bhūta = element (see II.18)
indriya = sense-organ (see II.18)
dharma = quality, here: form (from √*dhṛ* 'to hold')
lakṣaṇa = characteristic, here: time-variation (from √*lakṣ* 'to observe')
avasthā = condition (from *ava* + √*sthā* 'to stand')
pariṇāma = transformation (see II.15)
vyākhyāta = explained (see I.44)

By this are [also] explained the transformations of form, time-variation and condition [with regard to] the elements [and] sense-organs.

According to Patañjali, change is threefold: (1) the succession of qualities or forms of a substance (*dharma-pariṇāma*); (2) the chronological sequence itself, i.e. past, present and future (technically known as *lakṣaṇa-pariṇāma*) and (3) the over-all form of manifestation (or *avasthā-pariṇāma*). These three types of change are universal and apply to the phenomena of consciousness as much as to material objects and the sensory receptors by which we perceive them. To elucidate this difficult notion Vyāsa introduces the following concrete example: The substance clay may appear as either a lump of clay or a water jar. These are its external forms (*dharma*), and the change from the one to the other does not affect the substance (*dharmin*) itself. The clay remains the same. But the lump or jar do not only have a spatial existence, they are also placed in time. Thus the water jar is the *present* time-variation (*lakṣaṇa-pariṇāma*) of the clay. Its *past* time-variation was the lump of clay.

Its *future* time-variation will presumably be dust. Throughout this change in time, the substance remains identical. How does this change in time occur? This question is answered by the third type of change, that of the condition (*avasthā*) of a thing. Time is a succession of individual moments which imperceptibly alter the condition of the water jar; this is the well-known process of decay, or ageing.

If we substitute consciousness for the clay in Vyāsa's example, we find that emergence and restriction are the forms (*dharma*) of consciousness, each being connected with the three segments of time (past, present, future) and having its own rate of growth or decay.

III.14 *śānta-udita-avyapadeśya-dharma-anupātī dharmī*

śānta = quiescent (see III.10)
udita = uprisen (see III.12)
avyapadeśya = indeterminable (from *a* + *vi* + *apa* + √*diś* 'to point out')
dharma = form (see III.13)
anupātin = following, here: conform to (see I.9)
dharmin = form-bearer (from √*dhṛ* 'to hold')

The form-bearer [i.e. the substance] is [that which] conforms to the quiescent, uprisen or indeterminable form.

The substance is permanently present in, yet in a sense different from, its forms. The quiescent forms are those which *have been*, the uprisen forms are those which *are*, and the indeterminable forms are those which *will be*, i.e. which are at this point in time still latent possibilities. All three are related to the same substance or form-bearer. Vyāsa explicitly contrasts this view with the buddhist conception of *anātman* or inessentiality according to which there are only myriads of changing forms but no underlying substance. The three kinds of transformation can be regarded as different ways of looking at the change affecting a single substance.

III.15 *krama-anyatvaṃ pariṇāma-anyatve hetuḥ*

krama = sequence (from √*kram* 'to stride')
anyatva = lit. 'other-ness', here: differentiation (from *anya* 'other' + *tva*)
pariṇāma = transformation (see II.15)
anyatva = here: differentiation (see above)
hetu = cause, here: reason (see II.17)

The differentiation in the sequence is the reason for the differentiation in the transformations.

'Sequence' means the temporal succession of forms of the same substance. This sequence is broken up into infinitely short intervals (*kṣaṇa*). If the flow of time were absolutely continuous, no change could ever occur. But at each moment in time, a subtle imperceptible (or perceptible only to the *yogin*) mutation takes place, and it is the accumulated effect of these minute changes of which we become aware. This interesting theory has its modern parallel in the conception of time not only as objective and relative but also as a discontinuous phenomenon. It is remarkable that Patañjali, probably inspired by his buddhist contemporaries, should have turned his mind to such complex philosophical issues which, by virtue of the incredible advances in micro-physics, are today recognised as constituting the most important problems in the philosophy of the natural sciences.

III.16 *pariṇāma-traya-saṃyamād-atīta-anāgata-jñānam*
pariṇāma = transformation (see II.15)
traya = triple, here: the three (see III.4)
saṃyama = constraint (see III.4)
atīta = past (from *ati* + √*i* 'to go')
anāgata = future (from *an* + *ā* + √*gam* 'to go')
jñāna = knowledge (see I.8)
Through constraint on the three [forms of] transformation [comes about] knowledge of the past and the future.

After the heavily theoretical aphorisms on the nature of change, Patañjali now returns to more practical matters. This *sūtra* is the first of a whole set which deals with the bonus effects resulting from the practice of constraint. The purpose of *saṃyama* is to prepare consciousness for its final termination through *asaṃprajñāta-samādhi* (see I.18). Therefore the special gifts acquired through the practice of constraint cannot possibly be stamped as unwanted side-effects which inevitably block the *yogin*'s path to Self-realisation. There is but one way to the ultra-cognitive enstasy, and this is *via* the practice of constraint. Irrespective of the object (idea) of concentration, the process of restriction in enstasy is in each case identical. The danger lies not in the extraordinary insight or powers which the practice of constraint is said to yield, but in the *yogin*'s attitude towards them. For, like any form of knowledge or power, these super-normal results can be misused or become ends in themselves. The popular opinion that these yogic abilities are not part of the path to Self-realisation is demonstrably wrong. The credit for making this important point goes to Professor C. Pensa. Writing about these powers (*vibhūti*), he emphasises that they *cannot* be 'separated from the essentially organic and unitary structure of Yoga'.[15]

III.17 *śabda-artha-pratyayānām-itara-itara-adhyāsāt-saṃkaras-tat-pravibhāga-saṃyamāt-sarva-bhūta-rūta-jñānam*

śabda = sound, here: word
artha = purpose, here: object (see I.28)
pratyaya = presented-idea (see I.10)
itara = other } here: one another
itara = other }
adhyāsa = superimposition (from *adhi* + √*as* 'to cast')
saṃkara = confusion (from *sam* + √*kṛ* 'to do')
tad = that, here: these
pravibhāga = distinction (from *pra* + *vi* + √*bhaj* 'to divide')
saṃyama = constraint (see III.4)
sarva = all
bhūta = element, here: being (see II.18)
rūta = language, here: sound (from √*ru* 'to roar')
jñāna = knowledge (see I.8)

[There is a natural] confusion of presented-ideas, object and word [on account of an erroneous] superimposition on one another. Through constraint upon the distinction of these [confused elements] knowledge of the sound of all beings [is acquired].

In everyday communication no distinction is made between, say, the word 'cow', the object 'cow' and the concept 'cow'. Conventional use blurs these differences, and it is only when we hear a foreign language that we are abruptly reminded that sound, object and idea are separate realities. We may repeatedly hear the Sanskrit word *go* and be able to identify it after some time, but unless we are shown the corresponding object, viz. a cow, we will never know its meaning (provided of course that we have no access to a translator's dictionary). The *yogin* makes a virtue out of our natural inclination to fuse and confuse these three distinct components by using it as a starting-point for an exercise in concentration and meditative-absorption and, finally, enstasy.

Whether or not it is literally true that the *yogin* can have

[15] C. Pensa (1973), p. 39.

knowledge of the language of all beings, only yogic practice can verify—or falsify. So long as we have no means of settling this question either way, it would seem advisable to suspend our judgement on the matter. This, of course, applies to all other claims made by the protagonists of Yoga.

III.18 *saṃskāra-sākṣāt-karaṇāt-pūrva-jāti-jñānam*

saṃskāra = subliminal-activator (see I.18)
sa-akṣa = lit. 'with eye', here: direct
karaṇa = lit. 'making' (from √*kṛ* 'to do'), here: perception
pūrva = previous
jāti = birth (see II.13)
jñāna = knowledge (see I.8)

Through direct-perception of subliminal-activators [the *yogin* gains] knowledge of [his] previous birth(s).

The subliminal-activators are the key to the past, since they have been formed by antecedent experiences. Direct-perception, or 'eye-witnessing' as the term *sākṣāt-karaṇa* may also be translated, is another way of describing the enstatic act of coinciding with the object (in this case the subliminal-activators).

III.19 *pratyayasya para-citta-jñānam*

pratyaya = presented-idea (see I.10)
para = other
citta = consciousness (see I.2)
jñāna = knowledge (see I.8)

[Through direct-perception] of [another's] presented-idea, knowledge of another's consciousness [is obtained].

This aphorism is best read in conjunction with the next *sūtra*.

III.20 *na ca tat-sa-ālambanaṃ tasya-aviṣayī-bhūtatvāt*

na = not
ca = and, here: but
tad = that
sa-ālambana = with support (see I.10)
tasya = of this, here: its (see I.27)
aviṣayin = lit. 'non-objective', here: being absent from (see I.11)
bhūtatva = lit. 'being-ness', here: being (from √*bhū* 'to become')

But [this knowledge] does not [have as its object] that [presented-idea] together with the [respective] support [i.e. object], because of its being absent from [the other's consciousness].

Direct-perception of another's presented-ideas, through the practice of constraint, discloses the consciousness of that person in its entirety. However, this supra-knowledge does not extend to the external object or objects on which those presented-ideas may be based.

III.21 *kāya-rūpa-saṃyamāt-tad-grāhya-śakti-stambhe cakṣuḥ-prakāśa-asaṃyoge'ntardhānam*

kāya = body
rūpa = form
saṃyama = constraint (see III.4)
tad = that
grāhya = to be grasped, here: to be perceived (see I.41)
śakti = power, here: capacity (see II.6)
stambha = suspension (see II.50)
cakṣus = eye (from √*cakṣ* 'to appear')
prakāśa = brilliance, here: light (see II.18)
asaṃyoga = disconnection, here: disruption (see II.17)
antardhāna = invisibility (from *antar* + √*dhā* 'to put')

Through constraint on the form of the body, upon the suspension of the capacity to be perceived, [that is to say] upon the disruption of the light [travelling from that body] to the eye, [there follows] invisibility.

As we know today, the visibility of objects depends on the light which they reflect and which strikes the retina where it is translated into nerve impulses. These are conducted to the brain, where they undergo a further translation into proper 'percepts'. It is at this final stage of processing the light patterns received by the eye into full-fledged images, that the *yogin*'s interception occurs. We know from experiments in hypnosis that a person can be made *not* to see certain things which are objectively present. It seems that the Yoga masters of yore have anticipated our present-day sophisticated understanding of the neurophysiological basis of perception.

III.22 *sa-upakramaṃ nir-upakramaṃ ca karma tat-saṃyamād-apara-anta-jñānam-ariṣṭebhyo vā*

sa-upakrama = lit. 'with approach', here: acute (from *sa* + *upa* + √*kram* 'to step')
nir-upakrama = lit. 'without approach', here: deferred (from *nir* + *upakrama*)
ca = and
karman = action (also action-fruition, action-deposit), here: left untranslated
tad = that, here: thereon
saṃyama = constraint (see III.4)
apara-anta = lit. 'extreme end', here: death (from *a* + *para* + *anta* 'end')
jñāna = knowledge (see I.8)
ariṣṭa = misfortune, here: omen (from *a* + √*ṛṣ* 'to pierce')
vā = or

Karman **[is of two kinds]: acute or deferred. Through constraint thereon, or from omens, [the** *yogin* **acquires] knowledge of death.**

Every action, or rather volition, leaves behind a corresponding trace or 'seed' in the depth of consciousness where it awaits its fruition in the form of volitional activity (see II.12–14). The term *karman* can mean three different yet related things, viz. (1) volitional activity, (2) its action-deposit (*karma-āśaya*) and (3) the fruition (*karma-vipāka*) thereof. Fruition, again, is said to be of two types; it can be either in the process of actualisation or it can be latent (deferred). Through constraint on this pool of subliminal-activators the *yogin* can gain insight into the patterning of his individual life and, in particular, foresee its end. Such knowledge can also be obtained from omens. Augury has been a highly developed art in ancient India.

III.23 *maitry-ādiṣu balāni*

maitrī = friendliness (see I.33)
ādi = *et cetera*
bala = power

[Through constraint] on friendliness *et cetera*, **[he acquires] powers.**

This aphorism recommends constraint upon the great sentiments mentioned in I.33, namely friendliness, compassion, gladness and detachment, though according to Vyāsa the last-mentioned is not meant to be included in this practice.

III.24 *baleṣu hasti-bala-ādīni*

bala = power
hasti = elephant (from *hasta* 'hand')
bala = power
ādi = *et cetera*

[Through constraint] on powers, [he acquires] powers [comparable to those of] the elephant *et cetera.*

Vyāsa thinks that in this exercise, constraint is to be practised with regard to a concrete manifestation of power and not power in the abstract sense. Thus elephantine strength is gained through constraint on the power of the elephant, or the strength of the wind is acquired by constraint upon the power of the wind, and so on.

III.25 *pravṛtty-āloka-nyāsāt sūkṣma-vyavahita-viprakṛṣṭa-jñānam*

pravṛtti = activity (see I.35)
āloka = flashing-forth (see III.5)
nyāsa = lit. 'setting down', here: focusing (from *ni* + √*ās* 'to sit')
sūkṣma = subtle (see I.44)
vyavahita = concealed (from *va* + *a* + √*dhā* 'to put')
viprakṛṣṭa = distant (from *vi* + *pra* + √*kṛṣ* 'to draw')
jñāna = knowledge (see I.8)

By focusing the flashing-forth of [those mental] activities [which are sorrowless and illuminating] [on any object] knowledge of the subtle, concealed and distant [aspects of those objects] [is gained].

This aphorism, to be read in conjunction with I.35–6, describes what may be called the yogic way of doing research.

III.26 *bhuvana-jñānaṃ sūrye saṃyamāt*

bhuvana = world (from √*bhū* 'to become')
jñāna = knowledge (see I.8)
sūrya = sun (from *svar* 'heaven')
saṃyama = constraint (see III.4)

Through constraint on the sun [he gains] knowledge of the world.

Vyāsa explains 'world' as the totality of regions known to the mythological world-picture of which there are seven:

(7) *satya-loka* (region of truth)
(6) *tapas-loka* (region of austerity) } *brahma-loka*
(5) *jana-loka* (people's region)
(4) *mahar-loka* (region of the great *Prajāpati)*
(3) *mahā-indra-loka* (region of the great Indra)
(2) *antarikṣa-loka* (intermediate region extending to the pole star)
(1) *bhū-loka* (earth region, the world of man)

III.27 *candre tārā-vyūha-jñānam*

candra = moon (from √*cand* 'to shine')
tārā = star (from √*tṛ* 'to cross over')
vyūha = arrangement (from √*vyūh* 'to array')
jñāna = knowledge (see I.8)

[Through constraint] on the moon, knowledge of the arrangement of the stars.

III.28 *dhruve tad-gati-jñānam*

dhruva = pole-star (from √*dhṛ* 'to hold')
tad = that, here: their
gati = course, here: movement (see II.49)
jñāna = knowledge (see I.8)

[Through constraint] on the pole-star, knowledge of their movement.

The word *tad* obviously refers to the stars.

III.29 *nābhi-cakre kāya-vyūha-jñānam*

nābhi = navel (from *nābh* 'aperture')
cakra = wheel (from √*car* 'to move')
kāya = body
vyūha = arrangement, here: organisation (see III.27)
jñāna = knowledge (see I.8)

[Through constraint] on the navel wheel, knowledge of the organisation of the body.

The modern analogue of the 'navel wheel', also known as the 'wheel of the jewelled city' (*maṇipura-cakra*), is the solar plexus situated in the abdominal region. Needless to say that the yogic conceptions differ considerably from those of modern anatomy, because the former is based upon the subjective, phenomenological experience of the body and not on *post mortem* dissection.

III.30 *kaṇṭha-kūpe kṣut-pipāsā-nivṛttiḥ*

kaṇṭha = throat
kūpa = well
kṣudh = hunger (from √*kṣudh* 'to be hungry')
pipāsā = thirst (from √*pā* 'to drink')
nivṛtti = cessation (from *ni* + √*vṛt* 'to whirl')

[Through constraint] on the 'throat well', the cessation of hunger and thirst.

The 'throat well' is presumably the same as the later *viśuddha-cakra.*

III.31 *kūrma-nāḍyāṃ sthairyam*

kūrma = tortoise
nāḍī = duct
sthairya = steadiness (see II.39)

[Through constraint] on the 'tortoise duct', steadiness.

The 'tortoise duct' is one of the many *nāḍīs* through which the vital force (*prāṇa*) is held to circulate. Through constraint on this particular duct, the *yogin* achieves perfect immobility. Although Patañjali has knowledge of the *cakras* and *nāḍīs*, there is no evidence that he was also acquainted with the concept of *kuṇḍalinī-śakti*, the serpent power, which plays an important role in Tantrism and Haṭhayoga.

III.32 *mūrdha-jyotiṣi siddha-darśanam*

mūrdhan = head (from √*mūr* 'to become solid')
jyotis = light (from √*jyut* 'to shine')
siddha = perfected one (from √*sidh* 'to succeed')
darśana = vision (see I.30)

[Through constraint] on the light in the head, vision of the perfected ones.

A possible explanation of the phenomenon of the effulgence in the head is found in the *Mahānārayaṇa-Upaniṣad* (XI.10–12): 'Standing in the middle of this [body] is a minute fiery flame, rising up. [It is] radiant like a thunderbolt striking down from the middle of a black cloud, fine like the awns of rice, shining yellow, atom-like.'

III.33 *prātibhād-vā sarvam*

prātibha = flash-of-illumination (from *pra* + *ati* + √*bhā* 'to shine')

vā = or
sarvam = all

Or through a flash-of-illumination [the *yogin* acquires knowledge of] all.

Vyāsa styles this 'the preliminary form of the knowledge born of discernment; just as the light at dawn [heralds] the sun'. He also calls it the 'deliverer' (*tāraka*).

III.34 *hṛdaye citta-saṃvit*

hṛdaya = heart
citta = consciousness (see I.2)
saṃvid = understanding (from *sam* + √*vid* 'to know')

[Through constraint] on the heart [he gains] understanding of [the nature of] consciousness.

III.35 *sattva-puruṣayor-atyanta-asaṃkīrṇayoḥ pratyaya-aviśeṣo bhogaḥ para-arthatvāt sva-artha-saṃyamāt puruṣa-jñānam*

sattva = here: left untranslated (see II.41)
puruṣa = Self (see I.16)
atyanta = absolutely (from *ati* + *anta* 'end')
asaṃkīrṇa = unmixed, here: unblended (see I.42)
pratyaya = presented-idea (see I.10)
aviśeṣa = non-distinct, here: non-distinction (see II.19)
bhoga = experience (see II.13)
para = other
arthatva = purposiveness (see I.49)
sva = own
artha = object, here: purpose (see I.28)
saṃyama = constraint (see III.4)
puruṣa = Self (see I.16)
jñāna = knowledge (see I.8)

Experience is a presented-idea [which is based on] the non-distinction between the absolutely unblended Self and *sattva*. Through constraint on the [Self's] own-purpose [which is distinct from] the other-purposiveness [of Nature], knowledge of the Self [is obtained].

Although consciousness, even in its most subtle manifestation as *sattva*, and the Self are forever separate, this distinction is blurred in actual experience. Through nescience a false identity comes into being which conceals the true Self. Through constraint upon the autonomy of the Self as opposed to the 'other-purposiveness' or teleology of Nature, this false identity is recognised as what it is, and the Self appears on the horizon of the *yogin*'s transmuted consciousness.

III.36 *tataḥ prātibha-śrāvaṇa-vedanā-ādarśa-āsvāda-vārtā jāyante*

tatas = thence (see I.22)
prātibha = flash-of-illumination (see III.33)
śrāvaṇa = hearing (from √*śru* 'to hear')
vedanā = sensing (from √*vid* 'to know')
ādarśa = seeing, here: sight (from *ā* + √*dṛs* 'to see')
āsvāda = taste (from *ā* + √*svād* 'to taste')
vārtā = smell (from √*vṛt* 'to stir')
jāyante = are produced, here: occur (from √*jan* 'to beget')

Thence occur flashes-of-illumination [in the sensory areas of] hearing, sensing, sight, taste and smell.

As a side-effect of the practice of constraint mentioned in III.35, the adept's sensory capacities become greatly enhanced. His supersenses disclose to him hidden and remote objects and, as Vyāsa adds, they even allow him to penetrate the past.

III.37 *te samādhāv-upasargā vyutthāne siddhayaḥ*

te = these (see I.30)
samādhi = enstasy (see I.20)
upasarga = obstacle (from *upa* + √*sṛj* 'to emit')
vyutthāna = emergence, here: waking-state (see III.9)
siddhi = attainment (see II.43)

These are obstacles to enstasy [but] attainments in the waking-state.

This aphorism must not be interpreted as a general rejection of the paranormal powers acquired through the practice of constraint and similar techniques. Patañjali merely wants to qualify the immediately preceding statement which concerns a group of phenomena which occur as highlights during the *yogin*'s everyday life and *not*, as often maintained, in the enstatic state. Like all mental activities of the externalising consciousness, these special phenomena are held to be inimical to the cultivation of inwardness and enstasy. Those attainments which are part of the enstatic experience itself cannot be thought to be detrimental to spiritual progress. Naturally, they must ultimately also be renounced (see III.50) so that the superior form of enstasy can come about.

III.38 *bandha-kāraṇa-śaithilyāt-pracāra-saṃvedanāc-ca cittasya para-śarīra-āveśaḥ*

bandha = bondage, here: attachment (see III.1)
kāraṇa = cause (from √*kṛ* 'to do')
śaithilya = relaxation (see II.47)
pracāra = going-forth (from *pra* + √*car* 'to move')
saṃvedana = feeling, here: experience (from *sam* + √*vid* 'to know')
ca = and
citta = consciousness (see I.2)
para = other, another
śarīra = body (from √*śṛ* 'to support')
āveśa = entering (from *ā* + √*viś* 'to enter')

Through the relaxation of the causes of attachment [to one's body] and through the experience of going-forth, consciousness [is capable of] entering another body.

Here another miraculous ability of the accomplished *yogin* is briefly indicated, viz. the transference of consciousness into another body. Again, it is not clear whether this is to be taken literally or whether the well-known phenomenon of astral projection is hinted at. In the latter case the phrase *para-śarīra* would denote the subtle body rather than the physical body. Vyāsa settles for the literal interpretation. He explains that the causes of attachment of consciousness to the body are the subliminal-activators stored in the depth-memory.

III.39 *udāna-jayāj-jala-paṅka-kaṇṭaka-ādiṣv-asaṅga utkrāntiś-ca*

udāna = up-breath (from *ud* + √*an* 'to breathe')
jaya = mastery (see II.41)
jala = water
paṅka = mud
kaṇṭaka = thorn
ādi = *et cetera*
asaṅga = non-adhesion (from *a* + √*sañj* 'to adhere')
utkrānti = rising (from *ud* + √*kram* 'to step')
ca = and

Through mastery of the up-breath [the *yogin* gains the power of] non-adhesion to water, mud or thorns and [the power of] rising.

The flow of the vital force (*prāṇa*) in the body is traditionally divided into five major areas of functioning:

(1) *prāṇa*—heart region
(2) *samāna*—abdominal area
(3) *apāna*—pelvic region and legs
(4) *udāna*—head and neck
(5) *vyāna*—pervading all parts of the body

This particular classification is according to the *Amṛtanāda-Upaniṣad* (34). Many other versions are known, and there is no absolute unanimity about the precise location and function of each class of vital force.

Subjugation of the up-breath empowers the adept to rise physically, that is, levitate. Vyāsa, moreover, understands the term *utkrānti* as the ascension of consciousness at the time of death.

III.40 *samāna-jayāj-jvalanam*

samāna = mid-breath (from *sam* + √*an* 'to breathe')
jaya = mastery (see II.41)
jvalana = effulgence (from √*jval* 'to blaze')

Through mastery of the mid-breath [he acquires] effulgence.

Vyāsa explains this as the kindling of the fire in the body, that is, the induction of psychosomatic heat.

III.41 *śrotra-ākāśayoḥ saṃbandha-saṃyamād-divyaṃ śrotram*

śrotra = ear (from √*śru* 'to hear')
ākāśa = ether (from *a* + √*kāś* 'to be visible')
saṃbandha = relation (from *sam* + √*bandh* 'to bind')
saṃyama = constraint (see III.4)
divya = divine (from √*div* 'to radiate')
śrotra = ear (as above)

Through constraint on the relation between ear and ether [he acquires] the divine ear.

This aphorism gives out another method by which 'divine hearing' (clairaudience) can be brought about. As we have seen, it comes spontaneously through constraint upon the idea of the special purposiveness of Nature and the autonomy of the Self (see III.35). The ether (*ākāśa*) is the medium through which sound is supposed to travel.

III.42 *kāya-ākāśayoḥ saṃbandha-saṃyamāl-laghu-tūla-samāpatteś-ca-ākāśa-gamanam*

kāya = body
ākāśa = ether (see III.41)
saṃbandha = relation (see III.41)
saṃyama = constraint (see III.4)
laghu = light
tūla = cotton
samāpatti = coincidence (see I.41)
ca = and
ākāśa = ether (see III.41)
gamana = traversing (from √*gam* 'to go')

Through constraint on the relation between body and ether and through the coincidence [of consciousness] with light [objects], such as cotton, [he obtains the power of] traversing the ether.

Ether is conceived as a kind of all-pervasive energised space surrounding all solids. Through the practice of constraint upon the relation between body and ether, the *yogin*'s consciousness is said to begin to coincide with the condition of lightness characteristic of such things as a piece of cotton, etc., as a result of which he gains the ability to move about freely in the ether. Again, Vyāsa and the other exegetes insist that it is the *yogin*'s physical body which becomes capable of countermining the law of gravity.

III.43 *bahir-akalpitā vṛttir-mahā-videha tataḥ prakāśa-āva raṇa-kṣayaḥ*

bahis = external
akalpita = formless, here: non-imaginary (from *a* + √*kḷp* 'to befit')
vṛtti = fluctuation (see I.2)
mahant = great
videha = incorporeal (see I.19)
tatas = thence (see I.22), here: from which
prakāśa = light (see II.18)
āvaraṇa = covering (see II.52)
kṣaya = dwindling (see II.28)

An external, non-imaginary fluctuation [of consciousness] is the 'great incorporeal' from which [comes] the dwindling of the coverings of the [inner] light.

Vyāsa distinguishes between an outer fluctuation of consciousness which abides in the body, and an outer fluctuation which is externalised. The former is called *kalpita* (lit. 'formed'), the latter *akalpita* ('formless'). He explains that the formless type is achieved by means of the first kind and that it is a concentration (*dhāraṇā*). What seems to be intended here is the projection of consciousness outside the body, first as an imaginary (*kalpita*) exercise, and then as the actual, non-imaginary (*akalpita*) externalisation of consciousness. As Vācaspati Miśra elucidates, this is not only for the purpose of entering another body, but also for reducing the misconceptions surrounding the nature of consciousness.

III.44 *sthūla-sva-rūpa-sūkṣma-anvaya-arthavattva-saṃyamād-bhūta-jayaḥ*

sthūla = coarse
sva = own
rūpa = form
sūkṣma = subtle (see I.44)
anvaya = connected, here: connectedness (see III.9)
arthavattva = purposiveness (from *artha* + *vat* + *tva*)
saṃyama = constraint (see III.4)
bhūta = element (see II.18)
jaya = mastery (see II.41)

Through constraint on the coarse, the own-form, the subtle, the connectedness and the purposiveness [of objects] [the *yogin* gains] mastery over the elements.

Nature is a multi-level, hierarchic structure. The coarse level of a thing is that aspect of it which can be perceived by the sense organs. The natural philosophy of Yoga knows of five categories of elements (*bhūta*) which together compose what is regarded as the coarse level of Nature. But these coarse objects have also a hidden dimension not immediately perceptible. First, there is what is technically referred to as the 'own-form' (*sva-rūpa*) of a thing; this is its characteristic essence, e.g. solidity for earth, liquidity for water, mobility for air, and so on. Second, there is the so-called subtle dimension of a thing which is its cause on the next deeper level. In the case of the elements these are, according to Vyāsa, the *tanmātras* or potentialities. 'Connectedness', in Vyāsa's opinion, stands for the primary-constituents (*guṇa*) of Nature which are common to all things. Finally, 'purposiveness' is the teleology immanent in these primary-constituents inasmuch as they serve the Self, be it in the form of world experience or release from it. Through constraint upon these five interconnected aspects of prakṛtic reality, the *yogin* learns to control the elements. What exactly this mastery consists in is described in the next aphorism.

III.45 *tato'ṇima-ādi-prādurbhāvaḥ kāya-saṃpat-tad-dharma-anabhighātaś-ca*

tatas = thence (see I.22)
aṇiman = atomisation
ādi = *et cetera*
prādurbhāva = manifestation (see III.9)
kāya = body
saṃpad = perfection (from *sam* + √*pad* 'to fall')
tad = that, here: its
dharma = constituent (see III.13)
anabhighāta = indestructibility (see II.48)
ca = and

Thence [results] the manifestation [of the powers], such as atomisation *et cetera*, perfection of the body and the indestructibility of its constituents.

Yogic tradition knows of eight supreme powers (*siddhi*) which are the mark of adepthood in Yoga. According to the *Yoga-Bhāṣya* these are:

(1) *aṇiman*—atomisation, i.e. the miniaturisation of the body
(2) *mahiman*—magnification, i.e. the power to expand infinitely
(3) *laghiman*—levitation
(4) *prāpti*—extension, i.e. the power to reach everywhere
(5) *prākāmya*—freedom of will
(6) *vaśitva*—mastery over the entire creation
(7) *īśitṛtva*—the power of creation
(8) *kāmāvasāyitva*—the power of wish fulfilment.

Generally all these astounding abilities are ascribed to the physical body, but according to a more sceptical and credible tradition the supra-normal powers pertain to the subtle body (see *Mahābhārata* XII.318.7) which we can tentatively equate with consciousness.

III.46 *rūpa-lāvaṇya-bala-vajra-saṃhananatvāni kāya-saṃpat*

rūpa = form, here: beauty
lāvaṇya = gracefulness (from √*lū* 'to cut' + *nya*)
bala = strength
vajra = thunderbolt, here: adamant (from √*vaj* 'to be strong')

saṃhananatva = robustness (from *sam* + √*han* 'to strike' + *na* + *tva*)
kāya = body
saṃpad = perfection (see III.45)

Beauty, gracefulness and adamant robustness [constitute] the perfection of the body.

This aphorism simply lists the qualities of the perfected body created through the practice of constraint mentioned in III.44.

III.47 *grahaṇa-sva-rūpa-asmitā-anvaya-arthavattva-saṃyamād-indriya-jayaḥ*

grahaṇa = grasping, here: process-of-perception (see I.41)
sva = own
rūpa = form
asmitā = I-am-ness (see I.17)
anvaya = connectedness (see III.9)
arthavattva = purposiveness (see III.44)
saṃyama = constraint (see III.4)
indriya = sense-organ (see II.18)
jaya = mastery (see II.41)

Through constraint on the process-of-perception, the own-form, I-am-ness, connectedness and purposiveness [he gains] mastery over the sense-organs.

The complex practice of constraint described in III.44 can also be applied to the sensory apparatus which represents the coarse level of a whole hierarchy. Its essence (*sva-rūpa*) is, like the *sattva* part of consciousness, brightness or luminosity. Its cause or subtle aspect is the principle of individuation or I-am-ness.

III.48 *tato mano-javitvaṃ vikaraṇa-bhāvaḥ pradhāna-jayaś-ca*

tatas = thence (see I.22)
manas = mind (see I.35)
javitva = fleetness (from √*jū* 'to urge' + *i* + *tva*)
vikaraṇa = organ-less, here: lacking sense-organ (from *vi* + √*kṛ* 'to make'
bhāva = condition, here: state (see III.45)
pradhāna = foundation, here: matrix (from *pra* + √*dhā* 'to put')
jaya = mastery (see II.41)
ca = and

Thence [comes about] fleetness [as of the] mind, the state lacking sense-organs and the mastery over the matrix [of Nature].

As a further consequence of the afore-mentioned practice of constraint, the expert, by overcoming the inbuilt limitations of the senses, learns to pass instantaneously from one level of existence to another, up to and including the very foundation of Nature itself. Vyāsa calls these three perfections 'honey-faced' (*madhu-pratīka).*

III.49 *sattva-puruṣa-anyatā-khyāti-mātrasya sarva-bhāva-adhiṣṭhātṛtvaṃ sarva-jñātṛtvaṃ ca*

sattva = here: left untranslated (see II.41)
puruṣa = Self (see I.16)
anyatā = distinction (from *anya* 'other' + *tā*)
khyāti = vision (see I.16)
mātra = mere, here: merely
sarva = all
bhāva = state (see III.48)
adhiṣṭhātṛtva = supremacy (from *adhi* + √*sthā* 'to stand' + *tṛ* + *tva*)
sarva = all
jñātṛtva = lit. 'knowing-ness' (from √*jña* 'to know' + *tṛ* + *tva*) } here: omniscience
ca = and

[The *yogin* who has] merely the vision of the distinction between the Self and the *sattva* [of consciousness] [gains] supremacy over all states [of existence] and omniscience.

The vision of discernment, which is the highest form of enstasy (see II.26), bestows omnipotence and omniscience on the adept. In his effort to ascend to this elevated condition, the *yogin* must traverse the entire many-layered body of Nature, gradually gaining mastery over one level after another. Now there remains nothing unknown to him, and in his privileged position he can influence everything according to his will. But there is a catch 22 condition: In order to complete the process of Self-realisation, he must forgo all this knowledge and power by dissolving even the last trace of his finite consciousness. Indian folklore knows of numerous *yogins* who have failed to take this last step and, instead of reaching the Self, have become masters of the universe. This popular view is obviously based on a literal reading of the supernormal powers to which the practitioner allegedly gains access at this penultimate stage of the path. However, if this sort of explanation requires any refutation at all, it can be pointed out that the very application of these miraculous abilities presupposes the renewed externalisation of consciousness and consequently implies the immediate loss of the spiritual status of the ascetic and thus logically also the loss of the respective power.

III.50 *tad-vairāgyād-api doṣa-bīja-kṣaye kaivalyam*

tad = this
vairāgya = dispassion (see I.12)
api = also, here: even
doṣa = defect (from √*duṣ* 'to be impaired')
bīja = seed
kṣaya = dwindling (see II.28)
kaivalya = aloneness (see II.25)

Through dispassion towards even this [exalted vision], with the dwindling of the seeds of the defects [he achieves] the aloneness [of the power of seeing].

According to J. H. Woods, this renunciation has as its object the various categories of powers delineated at great length in the preceding aphorisms. But another, deeper, explanation is possible. In fact, it appears that what must be renounced is the vision of discernment (*viveka-khyāti*) itself. This is the higher form of dispassion (*para-vairāgya*) mentioned in I.16. This final act of renunciation concerns consciousness itself. It must be reduced to ashes, its seeds must be sterilised so as to render all future conscious activity impossible. What remains after this ultimate reduction is the Self itself. This coincides with the aloneness of the power of seeing, that is, emancipation.

III.51 *sthāny-upanimantraṇe saṅga-smaya-akaraṇaṃ punar-aniṣṭa-prasaṅgāt*

sthānin = occupying a high position, here: high-placed (from √*sthā* 'to stand')
upanimantraṇa = invitation (from *upa* + *ni* + √*man* 'to think' + *tra* + *na*)
saṅga = attachment (see III.39)
smaya = pride (from √*smi* 'to smile')
akaraṇa = here: no cause (from *a* + √*kṛ* 'to make')

punar = again, here: renewed
aniṣṭa = undesired (from *an* + √*iṣ* 'to desire')
prasaṅga = inclination (from *pra* + √*sañj* 'to adhere to')

Upon the invitation of high-placed [beings], [he should give himself] no cause for attachment or pride, because of the renewed and undesired inclination [for lower levels of existence].

Here Patañjali takes us a few steps back again from the heights of Self-realisation, namely to the level of cognitive enstasy. The *yogin* who is accomplished in the practice of the object-oriented modes of enstasy may find that he encounters discarnate beings (gods, angels) who may unintentionally deflect his single-mindedness by offering him all manners of promising distractions. These are the joys of heaven which the seeker for Self-realisation has renounced at the very outset of his spiritual life (see I.15).

III.52 *kṣaṇa-tat-kramayoḥ saṃyamād-viveka-jaṃ jñānam*

kṣaṇa = moment (see III.9)
tad = this, here: its
krama = sequence (see III.15)
saṃyama = constraint (see III.4)
viveka = discernment (see II.26)
ja = born (from √*jan* 'to beget')
jñāna = knowledge, here: gnosis (see I.8)

Through constraint on the moment [of time] and its sequence [he obtains] the gnosis born of discernment.

Yet another way of performing constraint is mentioned, viz. on the phenomenon of time, or rather its quantum, the so-called 'moment'. This will procure for the *yogin* that transcendental-knowledge which has as its essence the discernment between consciousness and root-consciousness (or Self).

III.53 *jāti-lakṣaṇa-deśair-anyatā-anavacchedāt-tulyayos-tataḥ pratipattiḥ*

jāti = birth, here: category (see II.13)
lakṣaṇa = time-variation, here: appearance (see III.13)
deśa = place, here: position (see II.31)
anyatā = distinction (see III.49)
anavaccheda = continuity, here: indeterminateness (see I.26)

tulya = similar (see III.12)
tatas = thence (see I.22)
pratipatti = obtainment, here: awareness (from *prati* + √*pat* 'to fall')

Thence [arises] the awareness of [the difference between] similars which cannot normally be distinguished due to an indeterminateness of the distinctions of category, appearance and position.

We distinguish objects by reference to three basic factors, viz. (1) the category or class to which they belong (apple/pear); (2) if they belong to the same class we consider their individual characteristics (red apple/green apple); (3) if both class and appearance are identical we nan still distinguish them on the basis of their spatial location (this red apple is next to that red apple). However, there are occasions when the ordinary mind perceives continuity where there is really discontinuity. A fitting example would be the presence of presented-ideas in the enstatic consciousness. Here the apparent duration of a specific presented-idea is an illusion. For, according to Patañjali's theory of the continual transformation (*pariṇāma*) of Nature, such stability is an impossibility. Upon analysis it is found that what seems to be a single presented-idea is in reality a whole series of presented-ideas of the same type. The application of constraint on the structure of time turns this theoretical understanding into experienced reality.

III.54 *tārakaṃ sarva-viṣayaṃ sarvathā-viṣayam-akramaṃ ca-iti viveka-jaṃ jñānam*

tāraka = deliverer (from √*tṛ* 'to traverse')
sarva = all
viṣaya = object (see I.11) } here: omni-objective
sarvathā = in every way
viṣaya = object (see I.11) } here: omni-temporal
akrama = non-sequence, here: non-sequential (see III.15)
ca = and
iti = thus, here: left untranslated
viveka = discernment (see II.26)
ja = born (see II.53)
jñāna = knowledge, here: gnosis (see I.8)

The gnosis born of discernment is the 'deliverer', and is omni-objective, omni-temporal and non-sequential.

At this highest level of enstatic realisation consciousness has *become* all things in all times. All objects and all time phases are experienced as one whole. Nothing remains to be known. Now consciousness has become so translucent that its transparency approximates that of the Self. Liberation is secured.

III.55 *sattva-puruṣayoḥ śuddhi-sāmye kaivalyam-iti*

sattva = here: left untranslated (see II.41)
puruṣa = Self (see I.16)
śuddhi = purity (see II.28)
sāmya = equality (from *sama* 'same')
kaivalya = aloneness (see II.25)
iti = thus, here: finis

With [the attainment of] equality in purity of the *sattva* and the Self, the aloneness [of the power of seeing is established]. Finis.

Self-realisation ensues, according to this aphorism, when consciousness in its most transparent aspect (as *sattva*) has reached a state of refinement comparable to the intrinsic purity of the Self. A stricter definition of emancipation is given in aphorism IV.34. It is possible that the present *sūtra* belongs to the *aṣṭa-aṅga* tradition where the metaphor of purity/purification is more conspicuous than in Kriyā-Yoga proper.

Upon abandoning the objects of knowledge the mind becomes dissolved. Upon the dissolution of the mind, [all that] remains is [the supreme state of] aloneness.
Haṭhayoga-Pradīpikā IV.62

Chapter Four
KAIVALYA-PĀDA

Also goal of yoga. Higher than Samadhi

Note: As the title suggests, the focal theme of this concluding chapter is *kaivalya* or, in Vācaspati Miśra's words, the analysis of the transmuted consciousness inclining towards final self-negation. However, the chapter contains much other incidental matter of a heavily philosophical nature. Many, though by no means all, of the ideas propounded have already been presented, or touched upon, in the preceding *pādas.* This gives this final chapter the general appearance of being a kind of résumé. Yet the apparent disjointedness of the discussion is deceptive. There runs a strong unitary line of thought through these aphorisms.

An important misunderstanding must be clarified right away. This is the erroneous assumption, originated by Vyāsa and naively followed by virtually all subsequent exegetes and translators, that the initial aphorisms (1–6) treat of a specific para-normal feat, viz. the ability to create 'artificial' consciousnesses. This profound misinterpretation has been much reinforced by the very first aphorism which, as Prof. J. W. Hauer has realised, must definitely be considered as an interpolation. However, my own research does not corroborate his hypothesis that the fourth chapter constitutes an entirely autonomous text. Its subject-matter, vocabulary and conceptual framework are demonstrably continuous with the preceding chapters of Patañjali's work proper.

IV.1 *janma-oṣadhi-mantra-tapaḥ-samādhi-jāḥ siddhayaḥ*
janman = birth (see II.12)
oṣadhi = herb

mantra = here: left untranslated (from √*man* 'to think')
tapas = ascesis (see II.1)
samādhi = enstasy (see I.20)
ja = born (see II.53), here: result
siddhi = attainment (see II.43)

The [para-normal] attainments are the result of birth, herbs, *mantra*[-recitation], ascesis or enstasy.

As we have seen, a substantial portion of the third chapter is dedicated to the topic of para-normal phenomena induced mostly through the practice of constraint (*saṃyama*). The present *sūtra* mentions enstasy as only one of several sources of those powers. Apparently they can also be acquired through such ascetic practices as fasting, standing stockstill, etc., or *mantra* recitation or herbs. In rare cases they may even be the direct result of a certain congenital aptitude. The use of herbal concoctions may seem surprising. Yet this tradition goes right back to vedic times and the ritual quaffing of the *soma* (fly-agaric?). At any rate, nowhere in the *Yoga-Sūtra* or any other Yoga scripture do we find the claim that drugs can replace the years of self-discipline and commitment demanded of the *yogin*.

IV.2 *jāty-antara-pariṇāmaḥ prakṛty-āpūrāt*

jāti = here: category-of-existence (see II.13)
antara = other (from *anta*), here: another
pariṇāma = transformation (see II.15)
prakṛti = nature, here: world-ground (see I.19)
āpūra = lit. 'over-flow', here: superabundance (from *ā* + √*pṛ* 'to fill')

The transformation into another category-of-existence [is possible] because of the superabundance of the world-ground.

According to the axiom that something cannot come out of nothing (see p. 16), new categories or forms of life must necessarily all be modifications of the same fundamental substratum, i.e. the world-ground. This is best conceptualised as a field of infinite possibilities, that is, as superabundance of potential forms which may come into actual existence in the course of time.

IV.3 *nimittam-aprayojakaṃ prakṛtīnāṃ varaṇa-bhedas-tu tataḥ kṣetrikavat*

nimitta = incidental-cause (from *ni* + √*mā* 'to measure')

aprayojaka = not causing, here: does not initiate (from *a* + *pra* + √*yuj* 'to yoke')
prakṛti = nature, here: process-of-evolution (see I.19)
varaṇa = choosing, here: possibility (from √*vṛ* 'to choose')
bheda = distinction, here: singling-out (from √*bhid* 'to split')
tu = but
tatas = thence (see I.22)
kṣetrikavat = like a farmer (from √*kṣi* 'to inhabit' + *ka* + *vat* 'like')

The incidental-cause does not initiate the processes-of-evolution, but [merely is responsible for] the singling-out of possibilities—like a farmer [who irrigates a field by selecting appropriate pathways for the water].

This obscure aphorism seeks to convey a basically quite simple idea whose implications, however, are rather more complex and deserve a deeper analysis than can be afforded to them here.

Nature (*prakṛti*) is a continuous process of creation and resorption of forms, a perpetual movement from potentiality to actuality and back to potentiality. This dynamism is inherent in Nature. But what are the mechanisms that channel this driving force, known as the primordial-will (*āśis*) (see IV.10), into the characteristic structures of the known universe? In other words, what are the incidental-causes? Vyāsa gives a strictly psychological (anthropocentric) answer: merit and demerit. Although it is true that Yoga is pre-eminently concerned with the life experience of the individual human being and his personal transcendence of life, the present aphorism is surely intended as a far more comprehensive statement. To make full sense of it we must, I think, identify the incidental-causes (*nimitta*) as the store of subliminal-traits (*vāsanā*). These are without beginning (see IV.10) and hence supra-individual. The personal subliminal-activators of a particular individual are thus merely a minute fragment of the total pool of subliminal-traits. It is this total network of forces rooted in the cosmic depth-memory which is co-extensive with the innate dynamism of Nature. The process of introversion and ultimate emancipation consists essentially in the progressive neutralisation or sterilisation of these canalising mechanisms.

IV.4 *nirmāṇa-cittāny-asmitā-mātrāt*

nirmāṇa = forming, creating, here: individualised (from *nir* + √*mā* 'to measure')

citta = consciousness (see I.2)
asmitā = I-am-ness (see I.17)
mātra = only, here: primary

The individualised consciousnesses [proceed] from the primary I-am-ness.

This is perhaps the most misunderstood of all the aphorisms. The cause of this confusion is the term *nirmāṇa-citta* which all interpreters, following the wrong cues of the *Yoga-Bhāṣya*, have taken to mean 'artificially created consciousness'. The *sūtra* is alleged to have been composed in reply to the question, arising from the treatment of the supra-normal powers mentioned in IV.1, as to whether the multiple bodies which the *yogin* can produce at will are also endowed each with a distinct consciousness. The classical answer to this is that the artificially created bodies must be thought to have their own separate consciousnesses as well.

But, as J. W. Hauer (1958) has shown, *nirmāṇa-citta* can have another, quite different, meaning. It can also simply denote the 'individualised consciousness', that is, the phenomenal consciousness as opposed to the root-consciousness or Self. In view of the philosophical context in which the present aphorism appears and also considering analogous conceptions in Yogācāra-Buddhism (of which Patañjali was very probably aware), this seems the more plausible explanation. How, then, must we interpret this *sūtra*? The answer to this question lies in the concept of *asmitā-mātra*. This is not merely the sense of identity which every individual possesses, but a deeper ontological principle which makes all individuation possible. In Sāṃkhya this is known as *ahaṃkāra* or 'I-maker'. It is that particular phase in the process of transformation from sheer potentiality to the manifest world, where subjective and objective world structures begin to emerge as separate. It is the matrix of all individual consciousness and of all external material objects.

IV.5 *pravṛtti-bhede prayojakaṃ cittam-ekam-anekeṣām*

pravṛtti = activity (see I.35)
bheda = distinction, here: distinct
prayojaka = causing, here: originator (see IV.3)
citta = consciousness (see I.2)
eka = one
aneka = other (from *an* + *eka*)

[Although the multiple individualised consciousnesses are engaged] in distinct activities, the 'one consciousness' is the

originator of [all] the other [numerous individualised consciousnesses].

This aphorism is generally translated along the following lines: It has been said that the creation of multiple bodies by means of the para-normal powers implies the simultaneous creation of multiple (artificial) consciousnesses. Yet, in order to avoid that these automata become independent the *yogin* has to create a kind of rally-point for them, a single, synthetic consciousness which feeds the other artificially created *cittas* with appropriate information. All this sounds very obscure and far-fetched. In the light of the above re-interpretation, a more realistic explanation can be offered. The 'one consciousness' is none other than the primary I-am-ness (*asmitā-mātra*) of aphorism IV.4. Even though the individualised consciousnesses are engaged in their several activities, that is, can empirically be seen to depend on their own sense of individuality, nevertheless the pre-individual I-am-ness is the source of them all.

IV.6 *tatra dhyāna-jam-anāśayam*

tatra = therein, here: of these (see I.13)
dhyāna = meditative-absorption (see I.39)
ja = born (see II.53)
anāśaya = without deposit (from *an* + *āśaya*, see I.24)

Of these [individualised consciousnesses] [that consciousness which is] born of meditative-absorption is without [subliminal] deposit.

If it were true, as Vyāsa contends, that this aphorism states that the artificially produced consciousness has no subliminal-deposit, one would have to assume major inconsistencies in the metapsychology developed by Patañjali. However, Patañjali tries to make an altogether different point. He speaks of the consciousness which has been transmuted through the practice of Yoga, the process of interiorisation which gains special momentum at the level of meditative-absorption. He does, of course, not state that meditative-absorption eliminates the subconscious deposits, but merely that it initiates a trend which is further accelerated by the enstatic states until its completion in *asaṃprajñāta-samādhi*.

IV.7 *karma-aśukla-akṛṣṇaṃ yoginas-trividham-itareṣām*

karman = action (see I.24), here: left untranslated

aśukla = not white
(from a + √*śuc* 'to be bright')
akṛṣṇa = not black
(from *a* + *kṛṣṇa* 'black')
} here: *neither* black *nor* white

yogin = here: left untranslated
trividha = threefold (from *tri* 'three' + *vidha*)
itara = other

The *karman* of the *yogin* is neither black nor white; [the *karman*] of others is threefold.

The term *karman* denotes here the moral consequences of one's actions or volitions in terms of meritorious and demeritorious subliminal-activators. *Karman* is traditionally divided into four categories:

(1) black (as found in a villain)
(2) white/black (as found in ordinary men whose deeds are partly meritorious and partly demeritorious)
(3) white (as found in pious persons)
(4) neither black nor white (as found in the adept *yogin*)

Since the entire volitional activity of the Yoga master consists in his abiding in the state of *asaṃprajñāta-samādhi*, no new subliminal-activators, either of a positive or a negative nature, can accrue to him. In this sense he can be said to have transcended morality as such. He is no longer within the compass of morality or immorality but has become an *a-moral* being.

IV.8 *tatas-tad-vipāka-anuguṇānām-eva-abhivyaktir-vāsanām*

tatas = thence (see I.22)
tad = that, here: of their
vipāka = fruition (see I.24)
anuguṇa = corresponding, here: which correspond
eva = only
abhivyakti = manifestation (from *abhi* + *vi* + √*añj* 'to display')
vāsanā = subliminal-trait (from √*vas* 'to abide')

Thence [follows] the manifestation [of those] subliminal-traits only which correspond to the fruition of their [particular *karman*].

This aphorism is meant to show the connection which exists between the consequences of an act in terms of retribution and the subliminal-traits. Both represent abstractions on different levels.

We can either say that a given volitional activity leaves behind a subliminal-trait which, in conjunction with other similar subliminal-traits, will (given time) have certain consequences for the individual; or we can say that by a given volitional activity the individual accumulates merit or demerit. The subliminal-activators which combine into traits are thus the very material of the action-deposit (*karma-āśaya*). They become manifest, that is, take effect in accordance with the moral quality of the antecedent volitional activity. What the term 'fruition' implies has been explained already (see II.13).

IV.9 *jāti-deśa-kāla-vyavahitānām-apy-ānantaryaṃ smṛti-saṃskārayor-eka-rūpatvat*

jāti = here: category-of-existence (see II.13)
deśa = place (see II.31)
kāla = time (see I.14)
vyavahita = concealed, here: separated
api = also, here: even though
ānantarya = succession, here: causal-relation (from *an* + *antar* + *ya*)
smṛti = memory, here: depth-memory (see I.6)
saṃskāra = subliminal-activator (see I.18)
eka = one } here: uniformity
rūpatva = lit. 'formness' (from *rūpa* + *tva*) }

On account of the uniformity between depth-memory and subliminal-activators [there is] a causal-relation [between the manifestation of the subliminal-activator and the *karman* cause], even though [cause and effect] may be separated [in terms of] place, time and category-of-existence.

We have encountered the idea of a depth-memory already in aphorism I.43. This concept seems to stand for the personal subconscious, that is, the chain of subliminal-traits connected with a particular individual rather than the total pool of subliminal deposits. It is because of the uni-formity (or identity) of the depth-memory and its component subliminal-traits pertaining to a specific individual that one person does not experience the fruition of the *karman* of another person. In other words, the subliminal-traits hang together in the form of a causal nexus irrespective of the span of time that may have elapsed between the moment of origination of a subliminal-trait and its taking effect. Nor, we are told, need the environmental setting be the same or even the form of existence. This means that the iron law of retribution holds not only with regard to one's present embodiment but extends to all one's future lives as well.

IV.10 *tāsām-anāditvaṃ ca-āśiso nityatvāt*

tāsām = of these, here: these (from *tad*)
anāditva = beginninglessness, here: without beginning (from *an* + *ādi* + *tva*)
ca = and
āśis = primordial will (from *a* + √*śās* 'to order')
nityatva = perpetuity (from *nitya* 'eternal' + *tva*)

And these [subliminal-activators] are without beginning because of the perpetuity of the primordial will [inherent in Nature].

The primordial will is Nature's supra-personal dynamism or 'urge' ceaselessly to transform itself, to actualise its inexhaustible potentiality in myriads of forms, both visible and invisible. There is no beginning to this process of alternating unfolding and resorption of the world structures, and hence there can also be no beginning to the subliminal-traits resulting from world experience by sentient beings.

IV.11 *hetu-phala-āśraya-ālambanaiḥ saṃgṛhītatvād-eṣām-abhāve tad-abhāvaḥ*

hetu = reason, here: cause (see II.17)
phala = fruit (see II.14)
āśraya = support, here: substratum (see II.36)
ālambana = support (see I.10)
saṃgṛhītatva = connectedness, here: connection (from *sam* + √*grah* 'to grasp')
eṣām = of these (from *etad*)
abhāva = disappearance (see I.10)
tad = that, here: of these
abhāva = disappearance (see I.10)

Because of the connection [of the subliminal-traits] with cause, fruit, substratum and support, [it follows that] with the disappearance of these [factors], the disappearance [also] of those [subliminal-traits] [is brought about].

'Cause' stands for nescience and the other causes-of-affliction (*kleśa*). 'Fruit' is the motive or purpose of action. 'Substratum' refers to consciousness and 'support' denotes the stimulus or object presented to consciousness. These are connected with the production and actualisation of subliminal-activators forming into subliminal-traits. These *vāsanās* cannot be directly eliminated, though their suspension is procurable indirectly by way of the gradual attenuation of the causes-of-affliction (see II.2; II.10–11).

IV.12 *atīta-anāgataṃ sva-rūpato'sty-adhva-bhedād-dharmāṇām*

atīta = past (see III.16)
anāgata = future (see II.16)
sva = own } here: as such
rūpatas = in form
asti = exists (from √*as* 'to be')
adhvan = path (from √*dhāv* 'to flow along')
bheda = here: difference (see IV.3)
dharma = property, here: form (see III.13)

Past and future as such exist, because of the [visible] difference in the 'paths' of the forms [produced by Nature].

Past and future are not phantoms, but have actual existence. The existence of the former time mode consists in those forms which, after having been actualised, have become pure potentialities again. Future, on the other hand, refers to the potential forms insofar as they may still be actualised. The passage of time can be read off on the ageing process of the individual forms. The reality of time is the reality of the ever self-modifying primary substance, viz. the world-ground or Nature (*prakṛti*).

IV.13 *te vyakta-sūkṣmā guṇa-ātmānaḥ*

te = these (from *tad*)
vyakta = manifest (see IV.8)
sūkṣma = subtle (see I.44)
guṇa = primary-constituent (see I.16)
ātman = self, here: composed of (see II.25)

These [forms] are manifest or subtle and composed of the primary-constituents.

The forms generated by Nature belong, as we have learned from aphorism II.19, to either of two major realms; they can be manifest or subtle. The latter category is the more comprehensive inasmuch as it includes everything except for the phenomena of the material level (see I.45). Vyāsa, however, understands the term *sūkṣma* as denoting past and future objects. Whichever interpretation is preferred, the meaning of the second half of the aphorism remains identical, namely that all forms of Nature, whether manifest or not, whether present or latent, have the primary-constituents for their essence (*ātman*).

IV.14 *pariṇāma-ekatvād-vastu-tattvam*

pariṇāma = transformation (see II.15)
ekatva = lit. 'one-ness', here: homogeneity
vastu = object (see I.9)
tattva = lit. 'that-ness' (see I.32)

The 'that-ness' of an object [derives] from the homogeneity in the transformation [of the primary-constituents].

If Nature is *process*, perpetual motion, how is it possible that objects appear to be stable and have a visible identity which sets them apart from one another? Patañjali's answer to this question is that the transformations of Nature are not arbitrary or uncontrolled but follow a pattern, whereby a given transformation 'repeats' itself so to speak and thus creates a homogeneous movement which then becomes experienceable as a distinct, unique object.

IV.15 *vastu-sāmye citta-bhedāt-tayor-vibhaktaḥ panthāḥ*

vastu = object (see I.9)
sāmya = sameness, here: singleness (see III.55)
citta = consciousness (see I.2)
bheda = difference, here: multiplicity (see IV.3)
tayoḥ = of both (from *tad*)
vibhakta = separation, here: separate (from *vi* + √*bhaj* 'to allot')
panthan = path, here: level (from √*path* 'to bring into')

In view of the multiplicity of consciousness [as opposed] to the singleness of a [perceived] object, both [belong to] separate levels [of existence].

The previous aphorism entailed a tacit refutation of the notion, propounded in the idealist school of later Buddhism, that the objects are products of the mind, having no existence in themselves. Patañjali's position is that consciousness and objective reality belong to different levels of existence. He points out that the same object is experienced by many consciousnesses, although we need not assume that their experiences of that object are all alike.

IV.16 *na ca-eka-citta-tantraṃ vastu tad-apramāṇakaṃ tadā kiṃ syāt*

na = not
ca = and
eka = one, here: single
citta = consciousness (see I.2)
tantra = dependent (from √*tan* 'to extend')
vastu = object (see I.9)
tad = that, here: this
apramāṇaka = unprovable (from *a* + *pra* + √*mā* 'to measure' + *na* + *ka*)
tadā = then, here: besides
kim = what?
syāt = could be (from √*as* 'to be')

And the object is not dependent on a single consciousness; this is unprovable; besides, what could [such an imaginary object possibly] be?

This aphorism is missing in some of the manuscripts, and it is possible that it belonged originally to Vyāsa's commentary. It merely reaffirms Patañjali's realist position. He rejects all forms of idealism or mentalism which deny objects a separate existence. Patañjali wonders how one could possibly speak of an object if it is asserted that it is nothing but an idea in the One Mind? Attention is selective and only a certain part of a given object is ever revealed to consciousness; hence one may ask what sort of existence the unperceived parts of the object have. How can we have knowledge of such objects at all if they are co-extensive with the ideas in our mind?

IV.17 *tad-uparāga-apekṣitvāc-cittasya vastu jñāta-ajñātam*

tad = that
uparāga = colouration (from *upa* + √*raj* 'to be excited')
apekṣitva = requisiteness, here: required (from *apa* + √*īkṣ* 'to look' + *tva*)
citta = consciousness (see I.2)
vastu = object (see I.9)
jñāta = known (from √*jña* 'to know')
ajñāta = not known (from *a* + √*jña*)

An object is known or not known by reason of the required coloration of consciousness by that [object].

Vyāsa compares the object with a magnet and consciousness with a piece of iron which is attracted to the object and held captive by it. A thing becomes known when it affects or colours the percipient consciousness.

IV.18 *sadā jñātās-citta-vṛttayas-tat-prabhoḥ puruṣasya-apariṇāmitvāt*

sadā = always
jñāta = known (see IV.17)
citta = consciousness (see I.2)
vṛtti = fluctuation (see I.2)
tad = that, here: their
prabhu = superior (from *pra* + √*bhū* 'to become')
puruṣa = Self (see I.16)
apariṇāmitva = immutability (from *a* + *pari* + √*ṇam* 'to bend')

The fluctuations of consciousness are always known by their 'superior', because of the immutability of the Self.

Consciousness cannot become conscious of itself. The experience of self-awareness is entirely due to the fact that the movements of consciousness are always apperceived by the Self. In other words, consciousness functions against the still background of the root-consciousness.

IV.19 *na tat-sva-ābhāsaṃ dṛśyatvāt*

na = not, here: no
tad = that
sva = own } here: self-luminosity
ābhāsa = luminosity (from *ā* + √*bhās* 'to shine')
dṛśyatva = lit. 'seen-ness', here: object-character (from √*dṛś* 'to see')

That [consciousness] has no self-luminosity because of [its] object-character.

The lustre of consciousness is merely borrowed from the light of the Self, for consciousness is like an object to the root-consciousness which apperceives it continuously. The Self is the ultimate foundation of the processes of perception. Without its presence, *citta* would be incapable of illuminating external objects.

IV.20 *eka-samaye ca-ubhaya-anavadhāraṇam*

eka = one } here: simultaneously
samaya = lit. 'coming-together' (see II.31)

ca = and
ubhaya = both
anavadhāraṇa = non-cognition, here: impossibility-of-cognising (from *an* + *ava* + √*dhṛ* 'to hold')

And [this implies] the impossibility-of-cognising both [consciousness and object] simultaneously.

Consciousness cannot be aware of itself and the object at the same time. According to Patañjali, the function of consciousness is restricted to the illumination, that is cognition, of objects, whilst its own processes are, in turn, apperceived by the transcendental Self. The root-consciousness, however, is perfectly self-luminous and cannot become the object of any other, extraneous, consciousness.

IV.21 *citta-antara-dṛśye buddhi-buddher-atiprasaṅgaḥ smṛti-saṃkaraś-ca*

citta = consciousness (see I.2)
antara = another (see IV.2)
dṛśya = seen, here: perceived (see II.17)
buddhi = cognition (from √*budh* 'to be aware')
buddhi = cognition
atiprasaṅga = lit. 'excessive connectedness', here: regress (from *ati* + *pra* + √*sañj* 'to adhere')
smṛti = memory (see I.6)
saṃkara = confusion (see III.17)
ca = and

If consciousness [were] perceived by another [consciousness], [this would lead to an infinite] regress from cognition to cognition and the confusion of memory.

Those who reject the idea of a perfectly self-luminous principle which cognises (apperceives) the contents of consciousness are forced to postulate an endless series of consciousnesses each apperceived by another. Patañjali discards this alternative as logically unsatisfactory and also because this kind of regress from consciousness to consciousness would lead to a breakdown of the functions of memory.

IV.22 *citer-apratisaṃkramāyās-tad-ākāra-āpattau sva-buddhi-saṃvedanam*

citi = transcendental-awareness (from √*cit* 'to be aware')
apratisaṃkrama = immobile, here: unchanging

tad = that
ākāra = shape (from *a* + √*kṛ* 'to make')
āpatti = occurrence, here: assumes (from *a* + √*pat* 'to fall')
sva = own, here: one's own
buddhi = cognition (see IV.21)
saṃvedana = experience (see III.38)

When the unchanging transcendental-awareness assumes the shape of that [consciousness], experience of one's own cognitions [becomes possible].

Self-consciousness is possible only because of the proximity of the Self. Although Self and consciousness are forever unmixed (see III.35), there is a 'sympathetic' relation between them which Patañjali characterises as one of conformity (*sārūpya*) (see I.4). He also uses the term 'correlation' (*saṃyoga*) (see II.17) to describe the apparent loss of the Self's autonomy and its equally apparent identification with a particular consciousness. In reality, however, the Self suffers no change or diminution. The apperception of consciousness on the part of the Self is not a series of acts performed by the Self, but is the very essence of the root-consciousness.

IV.23 *draṣṭṛ-dṛśya-uparaktaṃ cittaṃ sarva-artham*

draṣṭṛ = seer (see I.3)
dṛśya = the seen (see II.17)
uparakta = coloured (from *upa* + √*raj* 'to be excited')
citta = consciousness (see I.2)
sarva = all, here: any
artha = purpose, here: object (see I.28)

[Provided that] consciousness is coloured by the 'seer' and the 'seen', [it can perceive] any object.

From the frog perspective of the individual, finite consciousness, this correlation manifests itself as a 'coloration' (*uparāga*) of consciousness by the Self. Conscious experience is based on a complete reversal of the true relationship between Self and consciousness. Out of nescience the latter arrogates to itself the role of subject, thereby lowering the Self to the status of an object. This erroneous reduction of the unchanging, eternal Self to the finite self-consciousness is one of two essential components of human consciousness. The other is the coloration of consciousness by the external objects.

IV.24 *tad-asaṃkhyeya-vāsanābhiś-citram-api para-arthaṃ saṃhatya-kāritvāt*

tad = that
asaṃkhyeya = countless (from *a* + *sam* + √*khyā* 'to be mentioned')
vāsanā = subliminal-trait (see IV.8)
citra = speckled (from √*cit* 'to be visible')
api = also, here: though
para = other } here: other-purposed
artha = purpose (see I.28) }
saṃhatya = combined (from *sam* + √*han* 'to strike'), here: collaborate
kāritva = activity (from √*kṛ* 'to do')

That [consciousness], though speckled with countless subliminal-traits, is other-purposed due to [its being limited to] collaborate activity.

It may seem that since all consciousness activity is continuously encoded and stored in the depth-memory in the shape of subliminal-traits serving as blueprints for future consciousness activity, consciousness is a kind of *perpetuum mobile*, entirely self-sufficient and existing for its own sake. This view is firmly disowned by Patañjali and all other Yoga and Sāṃkya thinkers. Consciousness, like all prakṛtic manifestations, exists for the sake of the Other (*para*), i.e. the Self. It cannot be otherwise, Patañjali argues, because consciousness is a composite process and, like all composite things, must necessarily serve another's purpose. Just as houses, tables and other similar composite objects do not exist for their own sake, so also consciousness and its contents have a purpose beyond themselves, namely the dual purpose of the Self's world experience or negation (see II.18). This argument is put forward as an ontological proof for the existence of the Self in the Yoga-Sāṃkhya metaphysical traditions.

IV.25 *viśeṣa-darśina ātma-bhāva-bhāvanā-vinivṛttiḥ*

viśeṣa = here: distinction (see I.22)
darśin = seeing, here: he who sees
ātman = self (see II.5) } here: self-sense
bhāva = becoming, state-of-being (see III.9) }
bhāvanā = cultivation, here: projection (see I.28)
vinivṛtti = discontinuation (from *vi* + *ni* + √*vṛt* 'to whirl')

For him who sees the distinction [between *sattva* and Self]

[there comes about] the discontinuation of the projection of the [false] self-sense.

Vyāsa interprets the compound *ātma-bhāva-bhāvanā* as 'pondering upon one's own state of being' in the form of such questions as 'Who was I? Who am I? What will become of me?' etc. However, it is conceivable that these words hint at a more general psychic phenomenon, namely the continuous projection and experience of oneself as a finite consciousness. The state of discernment between one's rarefied consciousness (as pure *sattva*) and the Self, in *asaṃprajñāta-samādhi*, deletes the sense of self-awareness of the temporal consciousness just as all other contents of consciousness have been extirpated. In a sense, in this elevated state of being, consciousness is so attenuated as to be hardly present. It certainly cannot be thought to have much in common with the consciousness of everyday existence, or even with the consciousness of the lower forms of enstasy.

IV.26 *tadā viveka-nimnaṃ kaivalya-prāgbhāraṃ cittam*

tadā = then
viveka = discernment (see II.26)
nimna = concave, here: incline (from *ni* + √*nam* 'to bend')
kaivalya = aloneness (see II.25)
prāk = before, in front
bhāra = load, here: borne (from √*bhṛ* 'to bear') } here: borne onwards
citta = consciousness (see I.2)

Then consciousness [thus] inclined towards discernment, is borne onwards towards the aloneness [of the power of seeing].

When only the flimsiest film of nescience, in the shape of the highly refined consciousness (as *sattva*), conceals the Self, the process of interiorisation becomes irreversible. The transmuted, purified consciousness gravitates, by its own momentum, towards self-annihilation which is synonymous with Self-realisation.

IV.27 *tac-chidreṣu pratyaya-antarāṇi saṃskārebhyaḥ*

tad = that
chidra = gap, here: interval (from √*chid* 'to cut')
pratyaya = presented-idea (see I.10)
antara = other (see IV.2)

saṃskāra = subliminal-activator (see I.18)

In the intervals of that [involuting consciousness], other [new] presented-ideas [may arise] from the subliminal-activators.

At first the switch from cognitive to ultra-cognitive enstasy may only last for a few seconds at a time. The *yogin* needs to habituate consciousness by cultivating subliminal-activators of restriction (*nirodha-saṃskāra*) which will inhibit the subconscious forces responsible for the externalisation of consciousness (see III.9). Gradually, he learns to gain control over the emergence of presented-ideas and to abide in the state of contentless awareness for long periods. Then comes a point where the subliminal-activators of restriction outweigh those of emergence, and consciousness begins to dissolve completely. What remains is not unconscious stupor but the lucidity of the root-consciousness or Self.

IV.28 *hānam-eṣāṃ kleśavad-uktam*

hāna = cessation (see II.25)
eṣām = of these, here: their (from *etad*)
kleśa-vat = like cause-of-affliction (see I.24, *kleśa*)
ukta = spoken, here: described

Their cessation [is achieved by the same means] as described for the causes-of-affliction.

This aphorism relates back to II.10 where Patañjali explains the means of removing the causes-of-affliction in their subtle form, i.e. as subliminal-activators. The way he recommends is the so-called process-of-involution (*pratiprasava*) initiated by the practice of the vision of discernment (*viveka-khyāti*).

IV.29 *prasaṃkhyāne'py-akusīdasya sarvathā viveka-khyāter-dharma-meghaḥ samādhiḥ*

prasaṃkhyāna = elevation (from *pra* + *sam* + √*khyā* 'to appear')
api = also, here: even
akusīda = non-usurious (from *a* + *ku* + √*sad* 'to sit')
sarvathā = always (see III.54)
viveka = discernment (see II.26)
khyāti = vision (see I.16)
dharma = here: left untranslated (see III.13)
megha = cloud (from √*mih* 'to make water')
samādhi = enstasy (see I.20)

For [the *yogin* who is] always non-usurious even in [the state of elevation], [there follows], through the vision of discernment, the enstasy [designated as] '*dharma* cloud'.

Once the *yogin* has reached this uppermost echelon of being, his sole concern must be to keep his consciousness in the same translucent condition by renouncing even the slightest appetence for life. This is what is known as the higher dispassion (see I.16). The reward for this total negation of prakṛtic existence *per se* is the enstasy of the cloud of *dharma*. It is not clear what precisely the word *dharma* stands for in this context, but most assuredly not 'virtue' as some translators flatly render it. Perhaps Patañjali borrowed this phrase from certain *Mahāyāna* scriptures where the concept of *dharma-megha* figures prominently. Whatever its exact meaning might be in the framework of Classical Yoga, this enstasy definitely represents the consummate phase of *asaṃprajñāta-samādhi* and thus immediately precedes Self-realisation, or the aloneness of the power of seeing.

IV.30 *tataḥ kleśa-karma-nivṛttiḥ*

tatas = thence (see I.22)
kleśa = cause-of-affliction (see I.24)
karman = here: left untranslated (see I.24)
nivṛtti = discontinuation (see III.30)

Thence [follows] the discontinuation of the causes-of-affliction and of *karman*.

The 'cloud of *dharma*' enstasy dispels nescience and removes all the other secondary causes-of-affliction. It also destroys the entire store of subliminal-activators and thus the *karma*-deposit itself. Vyāsa maintains that this total annihilation of the very foundation of the empirical consciousness frees the *yogin* while yet alive. But this cannot be the same as the vedāntic conception according to which the *yogin*, having reached Self-realisation, to all intents and purposes continues with the business of life. The notion of liberation implicit in the metaphysics of Kriyā-Yoga is more radical. Here Self-realisation and world-involvement are diametrically opposed states of being. Therefore we must conclude that upon the attainment of the aloneness of the power of seeing, the *yogin* in fact ceases to exist as a human being. His body may live on for a period of time, though in a state of catalepsy, and before long goes the way of all finite things.

IV.31 *tadā sarva-āvaraṇa-mala-apetasya jñānasya-ānantyāj-jñeyam-alpam*

tadā = then
sarva = all
āvaraṇa = covering (see II.52)
mala = imperfection
apeta = removed (from *apa* + √*i* 'to go')
jñāna = knowledge, here: gnosis (see I.8)
ānantya = infinity (from *an* + *anta* 'end' + *ya*)
jñeya = to be known (from √*jña* 'to know')
alpa = little

Then, [when] all coverings of imperfection are removed little [remains] to be known because of the infinity of the [resulting] gnosis.

The finite, empirical consciousness can always only know one aspect of reality at a time, whilst all other aspects remain concealed from it. This is held to be due to the natural impurity or imperfection of consciousness (selective attention). However, when vacated from all conceptualising activity, consciousness reflects things as they are in themselves. Paradoxically, the more all conscious activity is restricted, the more comprehensive becomes knowledge or the scope of consciousness. By means of the vision of discernment, consciousness is rendered transparent and begins to approximate the omniscience of Self-awareness (see III.54). To avoid the impression that this knowledge is still, or again, conceptual knowledge, I have translated the term *jñāna* with 'gnosis', a kind of revelation where all things are reflected in consciousness and consciousness appears to be the essence of all things. It is difficult to tell whether we should still speak of consciousness or already of the root-consciousness.

IV.32 *tataḥ kṛta-arthānāṃ pariṇāma-krama-samāptir-guṇānām*

tatas = thence (see I.22)
kṛta = done, here: fulfilled (see II.22)
artha = here: purpose (see I.28)
pariṇāma = transformation (see II.15)
krama = sequence (see III.15)
samāpti = termination (from *sam* + √*āp* 'to reach')
guṇa = primary-constituent (see I.16)

Thence [comes about] the termination of the sequences in the transformation of the primary-constituents [whose] purpose is fulfilled.

At the peak of the ultra-cognitive enstasy, the *yogin's* individual cosmos comes to a standstill. As the Self awakens to its perpetual autonomy, the prakṛtic structures associated with, or rather constituting, the individual consciousness and bodily complex begin to disintegrate. The series of impulses which compose the incessant oscillations of Nature become disrupted, and in virtue of this localised stoppage of the vibrations of the primary-constituents, consciousness collapses, and the physical body soon meets with the same fate.

IV.33 *kṣaṇa-pratiyogī pariṇāma-apara-anta-nirgrāhyaḥ kramaḥ*

kṣaṇa = moment (see III.9)
pratiyogin = correlative (from *prati* + √*yuj* 'to join')
pariṇāma = transformation (see II.15)
apara = other } here: terminal point (see III.22)
anta = end }
nirgrāhya = ascertained (from *nir* + √*grah* 'to grasp'), here: apprehensible
krama = sequence (see III.15)

Sequence [means that which is] correlative to the moment [of time], apprehensible at the terminal-point of a [particular] transformation.

Patañjali describes in a nutshell the relation between the ultimate unit of time, the moment, and the ultimate unit of the continuous process of transformation, the sequence, as one of correlation. This atomistic conception foreshadows in certain respects contemporary ideas about the discontinuous nature of time and of the space-time continuum.

IV.34 *puruṣa-artha-śūnyānāṃ guṇānāṃ pratiprasavaḥ kaivalyaṃ sva-rūpa-pratiṣṭhā vā citi-śaktir-iti*

puruṣa = Self (see I.16)
artha = here: purpose (see I.28)
śūnya = void, here: devoid (see I.9)
guṇa = primary-constituent (see I.16)
pratiprasava = process-of-involution (see II.10)
kaivalya = aloneness (see II.25)
sva = own
rūpa = form
pratiṣṭhā = foundation, here: establishment (see I.8)

vā = or
citi = awareness (see IV.22)
śakti = power (see II.6)
iti = here: finis

The process-of-involution of the primary-constituents, devoid of purpose for the Self, is [what is called] aloneness [of seeing], or the establishment of the power of awareness in [its] own-form. Finis.

Upon Self-realisation, the primary-constituents of Nature are, teleologically speaking, of no further use to the Self. They cease to vibrate in the pattern characteristic of the *yogin*'s body and mind complex and become resolved into the unmanifest core (*prakṛti-pradhāna* = *aliṅga*). The power of awareness abiding in its natural state is of course none other than the self-luminous root-consciousness. Throughout the ups and downs in the life of the *yogin*, no change took place on the level of the Self. What seems like an unsurpassed achievement from the perspective of the finite consciousness, is an absolute non-event from the Self's viewpoint. For, the Self is by definition free, autonomous, sheer awareness and quite unaffected by any loss of identity or by any form of limitation.

The great drama of bondage and liberation is enacted entirely on the stage of the finite mind. The Self is at best a disinterested spectator of it all, unmoved by failure or success. As M. Eliade remarked appreciatively: 'It is impossible . . . to disregard one of India's greatest discoveries: that of consciousness as witness, of consciousness freed from its psychophysiological structures and their temporal conditioning . . .'[16]

[16] M. Eliade (1969²), p. xx.

CONTINUOUS TRANSLATION

. . . Yoga is full of facts of which the scientific background is as yet very imperfectly understood.

K. S. Joshi, 'On the Meaning of Yoga' (p. 53).

Samādhi-Pāda

I.1 Now [commences] the exposition of Yoga.

I.2 Yoga is the restriction of the fluctuations of consciousness.

I.3 Then the seer [i.e. the Self] abides in [its] essence.

I.4 At other times [there is] conformity [of the Self] with the fluctuations [of consciousness].

I.5 The fluctuations are fivefold; afflicted or non-afflicted.

I.6 [The five types of fluctuations are:] valid-cognition, misconception, conceptualisation, sleep and memory.

I.7 Valid-cognition [is based on] perception, inference and testimony.

I.8 Misconception is erroneous knowledge not based on the [actual] appearance of that [which is the underlying object].

I.9 Conceptualisation is without [perceivable] object, following [entirely] verbal knowledge.

I.10 Sleep is a fluctuation founded on the presented-idea of the non-occurrence [of other contents of consciousness].

I.11 Remembering is the non-deprivation of the experienced object.

I.12 The restriction of these [fluctuations] [is achieved] through practice and dispassion.

I.13 Practice is the exertion [in gaining] stability in that [state of restriction].

I.14 But this [practice] is firmly grounded [only after it has been] cultivated properly and for a long time uninterruptedly.

I.15 Dispassion is the knowledge-of-mastery of [that *yogin* who is] without thirst for seen [i.e. earthly] and revealed objects.

I.16 The superior [form] of this [dispassion] is the non-thirsting for the primary-constituents [of Nature] [which results] from the vision of the Self.

I.17 [The enstasy arising out of the state of restriction] is cognitive [i.e. object-oriented] by being connected with [the forms of] cogitation, reflection, joy or I-am-ness.

I.18 The other [type of enstasy] has a residuum of subliminal-activators; [it follows] the former [cognitive enstasy] upon the practice of the presented-idea of cessation.

I.19 [The enstasy of those who have] merged with the world-ground [and those who are] bodiless [is due to the persistence of] the presented-idea of becoming.

I.20 [The enstasy] of the others [i.e. those *yogins* whose path is described in I.18] is preceded by faith, energy, mindfulness, enstasy and supra-cognition.

I.21 [This supreme enstasy] is near to [him who is] extremely vehement [in his practice of Yoga].

I.22 Because [this vehemence can be] modest, medium or excessive, [there is] hence also a difference [in the proximity of the *yogins* to the supreme enstasy].

I.23 Or [enstasy is gained] through devotion to the Lord.

I.24 The Lord is a special Self [because he is] untouched by the causes-of-affliction, action [and its] fruition [and by] the deposit [in the depth-memory].

I.25 In Him the seed of omniscience is unsurpassed.

I.26 [The Lord] was also the mentor of the earlier [*yogins*] by virtue of [His] temporal continuity.

I.27 His symbol is the *praṇava* [i.e. the syllable *oṃ*].

I.28 The recitation of that [syllable] [leads to] the contemplation of its meaning.

I.29 Thence [follows] the attainment of [habitual] inward-mindedness and also the disappearance of the obstacles [mentioned below].

I.30 Sickness, languor, doubt, heedlessness, sloth, dissipation, false vision, non-attaining of the stages [of Yoga] and instability [in these stages] are the distractions of consciousness; these are the obstacles.

I.31 Pain, depression, tremor of the limbs, [wrong] inhalation and exhalation are accompanying [symptoms] of the distractions.

I.32 In order to counteract these [distractions] [the *yogin* should resort to] the practice [of concentration] on a single principle.

I.33 The projection of friendliness, compassion, gladness and equanimity towards objects—[be they] joyful, sorrowful, meritorious or demeritorious—[bring about] the pacification of consciousness.

I.34 Or [restriction is achieved] by [the controlled] expulsion and retention of the breath.

I.35 Or [restriction comes about when] an object-centred activity has arisen which holds the mind in steadiness.

I.36 Or [restriction is achieved by mental activities which are] sorrowless and illuminating.

I.37 Or [restriction is achieved when] consciousness is directed to [those beings who] have conquered attachment.

I.38 Or [restriction is achieved when consciousness] is resting on the insight [arising from] dreams and sleep.

I.39 Or [restriction is achieved] through meditative-absorption as desired.

I.40 His mastery [extends] from the most minute to the greatest magnitude.

I.41 [In the case of a consciousness whose] fluctuations have dwindled [and which has become] like a transparent jewel, [there results]—[with reference to] the 'grasper', 'grasping' and the 'grasped'—[a state of] coincidence with that on which [consciousness] abides and by which [consciousness] is 'anointed'.

I.42 [So long as there is] conceptual knowledge [based on] the intent of words in this [enstasy], [then this state is called] coincidence interspersed with cogitation.

I.43 On the purification of the depth-memory [which has become], as it were, empty of its essence, [and when] the object alone is shining forth—[then this state is called] ultra-cognitive [coincidence].

I.44 Thus by this [above-mentioned form of coincidence] [the other two types of enstasy]—[viz.] the reflexive and the ultra-reflexive—are explained; [these have] subtle objects [as props for concentration].

I.45 And the subtle objects terminate in the Undifferentiate.

I.46 These [kinds of coincidence] verily [belong to the class of] enstasy with seed.

I.47 When there is lucidity in the ultra-reflexive [enstasy], [then this is called] the clarity of the inner-being.

I.48 In this [state of utmost lucidity] insight is truth-bearing.

I.49 The scope [of this gnostic insight] is distinct from the insight [gained from] tradition and inference [owing to its] particular purposiveness.

I.50 The subliminal-activator born from that [gnostic flash] obstructs the other subliminal-activators.

I.51 Upon the restriction also of this [regressive subliminal-activator] [there ensues], owing to the restriction of all [contents of consciousness], the enstasy without seed.

Sādhana-Pāda

II.1 Ascesis, self-study and devotion to the Lord [constitute] Kriyā-Yoga.

II.2 [This Yoga has] the purpose of cultivating enstasy as also the purpose of attenuating the causes-of-affliction.

II.3 Nescience, I-am-ness, attachment, aversion and the will-to-live are the five causes-of-affliction.

II.4 Nescience is the field of the other [causes-of-affliction]; [they can be] dormant, attenuated, intercepted or aroused.

II.5 Nescience is the seeing of [that which is] eternal, pure, joyful and the Self in [that which is] ephemeral, impure, sorrowful and the non-self.

II.6 I-am-ness is the identification as it were of the powers of vision and 'vision-er' [i.e. the Self].

II.7 Attachment is [that which] rests on pleasant [experiences].

II.8 Aversion is [that which] rests on sorrowful [experiences].

II.9 The will-to-live, flowing along [by its] own-momentum, is rooted thus even in the sages.

II.10 These [causes-of-affliction], [in their] subtle [form], are to be overcome by the process-of-involution.

II.11 The fluctuations of these [causes-of-affliction] are to be overcome by meditative-absorption.

II.12 The causes-of-affliction are the root of the action-deposit, and [this] may be experienced in the seen [i.e. the present] birth or in an unseen [i.e. future] [birth].

II.13 [So long as] the root exists, [there is also] fruition from it: birth, life and enjoyment.

II.14 These [three] have delight or distress as results, according to the causes, [which may be] meritorious or demeritorious.

II.15 Because of the sorrow in the [continual] transformation [of the world-ground], [in] the anguish [and in] the subliminal-activators and on account of the conflict between the movements of the primary-constituents—to the discerner all is but sorrow.

II.16 [That which is] to be overcome is sorrow yet-to-come.

II.17 The correlation between the seer [i.e. the Self] and the seen [i.e. Nature] is the cause [of that which is] to be overcome.

II.18 The seen [i.e. Nature] has the character of brightness, activity and inertia; it is embodied in elements and sense-organs [and it serves] the [dual] purpose of enjoyment and emancipation.

II.19 The levels of the primary-constituents are the particularised, the unparticularised, the differentiate and the undifferentiate.

II.20 The seer [which is] the sheer [power of] seeing, although pure, apperceives the presented-ideas.

II.21 The essence of the seen [i.e. Nature] is only for the sake of this [Self].

II.22 Although [the seen] has ceased [to exist] for [the *yogin* whose] purpose has been accomplished, it has nevertheless not ceased [to exist altogether], since it is common-experience [with respect to all] other [beings].

II.23 The correlation [between the seer and the seen] is the reason for the apprehension of the own-form of the power of the owner and that of the owned [i.e. Nature].

II.24 The cause of this [correlation] is nescience.

II.25 With the disappearance of this [nescience] the correlation [also] disappears; this is [total] cessation, the aloneness of the [sheer power of] seeing.

II.26 The means of [attaining] cessation is the unceasing vision of discernment.

II.27 For him [who possesses this unceasing vision of discernment] there arises, in the last stage, transcendental-insight [which is] sevenfold.

*II.28 Through the performance of the members of Yoga and with the dwindling of impurity, [there comes about] the radiance of gnosis [which develops] up to the vision of discernment.

*II.29 Restraint, observance, posture, breath-control, sense-withdrawal, concentration, meditative-absorption and enstasy are the eight members [of Yoga].

*II.30 Non-harming, truthfulness, non-stealing, chastity and greedlessness are the restraints.

*II.31 [These are valid] in all spheres, irrespective of birth, place, time and circumstance [and constitute] the great vow.

*II.32 Purity, contentment, austerity, self-study and devotion to the Lord are the observances.

*II.33 For the repelling of unwholesome-deliberation [the *yogin* should pursue] the cultivation of the opposite.

*II.34 The unwholesome-deliberations, [such as] harming *et cetera*, [whether] done, caused to be done or approved, [whether] arising from greed, anger or infatuation, [whether] modest, medium or excessive—[these find their] unending fruition in nescience and sorrow; thus [the *yogin* should devote himself to] the cultivation of [their] opposites.

*II.35 When [the *yogin*] is grounded in [the virtue] of non-harming, [all] enmity is abandoned in his presence.

*II.36 When grounded in truthfulness, action [and its] fruition depend [on him].

*II.37 When grounded in non-stealing, all [kinds of] jewels appear [for him].

*II.38 When grounded in chastity, [great] vitality is acquired.

*II.39 When steadied in greedlessness [he secures] knowledge of the wherefore of [his] birth(s).

*II.40 Through purity [he gains] distance towards his own limbs [and also] [the desire for] non-contamination by others.

*II.41 [Furthermore:] purity of *sattva*, gladness, one-pointedness, mastery of the sense-organs and the capability for self-vision [are achieved].

*II.42 Through contentment unexcelled joy is gained.

*II.43 Through austerity, on account of the dwindling of impurity, perfection of the body and the sense-organs [is gained].

*II.44 Through self-study [the *yogin* establishes] contact with the chosen deity.

*II.45 Through devotion to the Lord [comes about] the attainment of enstasy.

*II.46 The posture [should be] steady and comfortable.

*II.47 [It is accompanied] by the relaxation of tension and the coinciding with the infinite [consciousness-space].

*II.48 Thence [results] unassailability by the pairs-of-opposites.

*II.49 When this is [achieved], breath-control [which is] the cutting-off of the flow of inhalation and exhalation [should be practised].

*II.50 [Breath-control is] external, internal and fixed in its movement, [and it is] regulated by place, time and number; [it can be] protracted or contracted.

*II.51 [The movement of breath] transcending the external and internal sphere is the 'fourth'.
*II.52 Thence the covering of the [inner] light disappears.
*II.53 And [the *yogin* gains] the fitness of the mind for concentration.
*II.54 Sense-withdrawal is the imitation as it were of the own-form of consciousness [on the part] of the sense-organs by disuniting [themselves] from their objects.
*II.55 Thence [results] the supreme obedience of the sense-organs.

Vibhūti-Pāda

*III.1 Concentration is the binding of consciousness to a [single] spot.
*III.2 The one-directionality of the presented-ideas with regard to that [object of concentration] is meditative-absorption.
*III.3 That [consciousness], [when] shining forth as the object only as if empty of [its] essence, is enstasy.
*III.4 The three [practised] together [on the same object] are constraint.
*III.5 Through mastery of that [practice of constraint] [there ensues] the flashing-forth of transcendental-insight.
*III.6 Its progression is gradual.
*III.7 [In relation to] the previous [five techniques of Yoga] the three [components of constraint] are inner members.
*III.8 Yet they are outer members [in relation to] the seedless [enstasy].
III.9 [When there is] subjugation of the subliminal-activators of emergence and the manifestation of the subliminal-activators of restriction—[this is] the restriction transformation which is connected with consciousness [in its] moment of restriction.
III.10 The calm flow of this [consciousness] [is effected] through subliminal-activators.
III.11 The dwindling of all-objectness and the uprising of one-pointedness is the enstasy transformation of consciousness.
III.12 Then again, when the quiescent and the uprisen presented-ideas are similar, [this is] the one-pointedness transformation of consciousness.
III.13 By this are [also] explained the transformation of form,

time-variation and condition [with regard to] the elements [and] sense-organs.

III.14 The form-bearer [i.e. the substance] is [that which] conforms to the quiescent, uprisen or indeterminable form.

III.15 The differentiation in the sequence is the reason for the differentiation in the transformations.

III.16 Through constraint on the three [forms of] transformation [comes about] knowledge of the past and the future.

III.17 [There is a natural] confusion of presented-ideas, object and word [on account of an erroneous] superimposition on one another. Through constraint upon the distinction of these [confused elements] knowledge of the sound of all beings [is acquired].

III.18 Through direct-perception of subliminal-activators [the *yogin* gains] knowledge of [his] previous birth(s).

III.19 [Through direct perception] of [another's] presented-idea, knowledge of another's consciousness [is obtained].

III.20 But [this knowledge] does not [have as its object] that [presented-idea] together with the [respective] support [i.e. object], because of its being absent from [the other's consciousness].

III.21 Through constraint on the form of the body, upon the suspension of the capacity to be perceived, [that is to say] upon the disruption of the light [travelling from that body] to the eye, [there follows] invisibility.

III.22 *Karman* [is of two kinds:] acute or deferred. Through constraint thereon, or from omens, [the *yogin* acquires] knowledge of death.

III.23 [Through constraint] on friendliness *et cetera*, [he acquires] powers.

III.24 [Through constraint] on powers, [he acquires] powers [comparable to those of] the elephant *et cetera*.

III.25 By focusing the flashing-forth of [those mental] activities [which are sorrowless and illuminating] [on any object] knowledge of the subtle, concealed and distant [aspects of those objects] [is gained].

III.26 Through constraint on the sun [he gains] knowledge of the world.

III.27 [Through constraint] on the moon, knowledge of the arrangement of the stars.

III.28 [Through constraint] on the pole-star, knowledge of their movement.

III.29 [Through constraint] on the 'navel wheel', knowledge of the organisation of the body.

III.30 [Through constraint] on the 'throat well', the cessation of hunger and thirst.

III.31 [Through constraint] on the 'tortoise duct', steadiness.

III.32 [Through constraint] on the light in the head, vision of the perfected ones.

III.33 Or through a flash-of-illumination [the *yogin* acquires knowledge of] all.

III.34 [Through constraint] on the heart [he gains] understanding of the [nature of] consciousness.

III.35 Experience is a presented-idea [which is based on] the non-distinction between the absolutely unblended Self and *sattva*. Through constraint on the [Self's] own-purpose [which is distinct from] the other-purposiveness [of Nature], knowledge of the Self [is obtained].

III.36 Thence occur flashes-of illumination [in the sensory areas of] hearing, sensing, sight, taste and smell.

III.37 These are obstacles to enstasy [but] attainments in the waking-state.

III.38 Through the relaxation of the causes of attachment [to one's body] and through the experience of going-forth, consciousness [is capable of] entering another body.

III.39 Through mastery of the up-breath [the *yogin* gains the power of] non-adhesion to water, mud or thorns and [the power of] rising.

III.40 Through mastery of the mid-breath [he acquires] effulgence.

III.41 Through constraint on the relation between ear and ether [he acquires] the divine ear.

III.42 Through constraint on the relation between body and ether and through the coincidence [of consciousness] with light [objects], such as cotton, [he obtains the power of] traversing the ether.

III.43 An external, non-imaginary fluctuation [of consciousness] is the 'great incorporeal' from which [comes] the dwindling of the covering of the [inner] light.

III.44 Through constraint on the coarse, the own-form, the subtle, the connectedness and the purposiveness [of objects] [the *yogin* gains] mastery over the elements.

III.45 Thence [results] the manifestation [of the powers], such as atomisation *et cetera*, perfection of the body and the indestructibility of its constituents.

III.46 Beauty, gracefulness and adamant robustness [constitute] the perfection of the body.

III.47 Through constraint on the process-of-perception, the own-form, I-am-ness, connectedness and purposiveness [he gains] mastery over the sense-organs.

III.48 Thence [comes about] fleetness [as of the] mind, the state lacking sense-organs and the mastery over the matrix [of Nature].

III.49 [The *yogin* who has] merely the vision of the distinction between the Self and the *sattva* [of consciousness] [gains] supremacy over all states [of existence] and omniscience.

III.50 Through dispassion towards even this [exalted vision], with the dwindling of the seeds of the defects [he achieves] the aloneness [of the power of seeing].

III.51 Upon the invitation of high-placed [beings], [he should give himself] no cause for attachment or pride, because of the renewed and undesired inclination [for lower levels of existence].

III.52 Through constraint on the moment [of time] and its sequence [he obtains] the gnosis born of discernment.

III.53 Thence [arises] the awareness of [the difference between] similars which cannot normally be distinguished due to an indeterminateness of the distinctions of category, appearance and position.

III.54 The gnosis born of discernment is the 'deliverer', and is omni-objective, omni-temporal and non-sequential.

III.55 With [the attainment of] equality in purity of the *sattva* and the Self, the aloneness [of the power of seeing is established]. Finis.

Kaivalya-Pāda

†IV.1 The [para-normal] attainments are the result of birth, herbs, *mantra* [-recitation], ascesis or enstasy.

IV.2 The transformation into another category-of-existence [is possible] because of the superabundance of the world-ground.

IV.3 The incidental-cause does not initiate the processes-of-evolution, but [merely is responsible for] the singling-out of possibilities—like a farmer [who irrigates a field by selecting appropriate pathways for the water].

IV.4 The individualised consciousnesses [proceed] from the primary I-am-ness.

IV.5 [Although the multiple individualised consciousnesses are engaged] in distinct activities, the 'one consciousness' is the originator of [all] the other [numerous individualised consciousnesses].

IV.6 Of these [individualised consciousnesses] [that consciousness which is] born of meditative-absorption is without [subliminal] deposit.

IV.7 The *karman* of the *yogin* is neither black nor white: [the *karman*] of others is threefold.

IV.8 Thence [follows] the manifestation [of those] subliminal-traits only which correspond to the fruition of their [particular *karman*].

IV.9 On account of the uniformity between depth-memory and subliminal-activators [there is] a causal-relation [between the manifestation of the subliminal-activator and the *karman* cause], even though [cause and effect] may be separated [in terms of] place, time and category-of-existence.

IV.10 And these [subliminal-activators] are without beginning because of the perpetuity of the primordial-will [inherent in Nature].

IV.11 Because of the connection [of the subliminal-traits] with cause, fruit, substratum and support, [it follows that] with the disappearance of these [factors], the disappearance [also] of those [subliminal-traits] [is brought about].

IV.12 Past and future as such exist, because of the [visible] difference in the 'paths' of the forms [produced by Nature].

IV.13 These [forms] are manifest or subtle and composed of the primary-constituents.

IV.14 The 'that-ness' of an object [derives] from the homogeneity in the transformation [of the primary-constituents].

IV.15 In view of the multiplicity of consciousness [as opposed] to the singleness of a [perceived] object, both [belong to] separate levels [of existence].

IV.16 And the object is not dependent on a single consciousness; this is unprovable; besides, what could [such an imaginary object possibly] be?

IV.17 An object is known or not known by reason of the required coloration of consciousness by that object.

IV.18 The fluctuations of consciousness are always known by their 'superior', because of the immutability of the Self.

IV.19 That [consciousness] has no self-luminosity because of [its] object-character.

IV.20 And [this implies] the impossibility-of-cognising both [consciousness and object] simultaneously.

IV.21 If consciousness [were] perceived by another [consciousness], [this would lead to an infinite] regress from cognition to cognition and the confusion of memory.

IV.22 When the unchanging transcendental-awareness assumes the shape of that [consciousness], experience of one's own cognitions [becomes possible].

IV.23 [Provided that] consciousness is coloured by the 'seer' and the 'seen', [it can perceive] any object.

IV.24 That [consciousness], though speckled with countless subliminal-traits, is other-purposed due to [its being limited to] collaborate activity.

IV.25 For him who sees the distinction [between *sattva* and Self] [there comes about] the discontinuation of the projection of the [false] self-sense.

IV.26 Then consciousness, [thus] inclined towards discernment, is borne onwards towards the aloneness [of the power of seeing].

IV.27 In the intervals of that [involuting consciousness], other [new] presented-ideas [may arise] from the subliminal-activators.

IV.28 Their cessation [is achieved by the same means] as described for the causes-of-affliction.

IV.29 For [the *yogin* who is] always non-usurious even in [the state of elevation], [there follows], through the vision of discernment, the enstasy [designated as] '*dharma* cloud'.

IV.30 Thence [follows] the discontinuation of the causes-of-affliction and of *karman*.

IV.31 Then, [when] all coverings of imperfection are removed little [remains] to be known because of the infinity of the [resulting] gnosis.

IV.32 Thence [comes about] the termination of the sequences in the transformation of the primary-constituents [whose] purpose is fulfilled.

IV.33 Sequence [means that which is] correlative to the moment [of time], apprehensible at the terminal-point of a [particular] transformation.

IV.34 The process-of-involution of the primary-constituents, devoid of purpose for the Self, is [what is called] aloneness [of seeing], or the establishment of the power of awareness in [its] own-form. Finis.

WORD INDEX TO THE YOGA-SŪTRA

All entries are in Sanskrit alphabetical order. However, participles are not classified under their verbal roots, but are listed separately; so are pronominal forms and negatives. The English words in brackets are those used in the actual translation and are not necessarily literal equivalents of the Sanskrit terms.

a

akaraṇa III.51 (no cause)
akalpita III.43 (non-imaginary)
akusīda IV.29 (non-usurious)
akṛṣṇa IV.7 (not black)
akrama III.54 (non-sequential)
akliṣṭa I.5 (non-afflicted)
aṅga I.31; II.40 (limb), II.28, 29 (member)
ajñāta IV.17 (not known)
ajnāna II.34 (nescience)
añjanatā I.41 (lit. 'anointment': anointed)
aṇiman III.45 (atomisation)
atad I.8 (not that)
atiprasaṅga IV.21 (regress)
atīta III.16; IV.12 (past)
atyanta III.35 (absolutely)
atha I.1 (now)
adṛṣṭa II.12 (unseen)
adhigama I.29 (attainment)
adhimātra II.34 (excessive)
adhimātratva I.22 (lit. 'excessiveness': excessive)
adhiṣṭhātṛtva III.49 (supremacy)
adhyātman I.47 (inner-being)
adhyāsa III.17 (superimposition)
adhvan IV.12 (path)
ananta II.34 (unending), II.47 (the infinite)
anabhighāta II.48 (unassailability), III.45 (indestructibility)
anavacchinna II.31 (lit. 'unseparated': irrespective of)
anavaccheda I.26 (continuity), III.53 (indeterminateness)
anavadhāraṇa IV.20 (impossibility-of-cognising)
anavasthitatva I.30 (instability)
anaṣṭa II.22 (not ceased)
anāgata II.16 (yet-to-come), III.16; IV.12 (future)

BIBLIOGRAPHY

I. Translations

Aprabuddha (1949/57), *The Science of Yoga* (Nagpur), 2 vols.
Bahm, A. K. (1967), *Yoga: Union with the Ultimate* (New York).
Bailey, A. (n.d.), *Light of the Soul* (New York).
Ballantyne, J. R. (1852), *The Aphorisms of the Yoga Philosophy of Patanjali* (Allahabad).
Bengali Baba (1949²), *Patanjala Yoga Sutra* (Poona).
Boissenain, J. W. (1918), *Yogasoetra's van Patanjali: Leerspreuken en eenheidsstreving* (Amsterdam/Haarlem).
Coster, G. (1934), *Yoga and Western Psychology* (London).
Covell, A. (1909), *Concentration* (London).
Deussen, P. (1899), *Allgemeine Geschichte der Philosophie* (Leipzig), vol. I.3.
Dvivedī, M. N. (1890), *The Yoga-Sūtras of Patañjali* (Madras).
Gherwal, R. S. (1935), *Patanjali's Raja Yoga* (Santa Barbara).
Hauer, J. W. (1958), *Der Yoga* (Stuttgart).
Isbert, O. A. (1955), *Rājayoga* (Gelnhausen).
Jhā, G. (1907), *The Yoga Darśana* (Bombay).
Johnston, C. (1912), *The Yoga Sutras of Patanjali* (New York).
Judge, W. (1920), *The Yoga Aphorisms of Patanjali* (Los Angeles).
Mangoldt, U. von (1957), *So spricht das Yoga-Sutra des Patanjali* (München).
Mitra, R. L. (1881–3), *Yoga Aphorisms of Patañjali, with the Commentary of Bhoja Rāja* (Calcutta), Bibliotheca Indica XCIII.
Prasada, R. (1912), *Patanjali's Yoga Sūtras* (Allahabad), Sacred Books of the Hindus IV.
Raghavan, V. (1956), *The Indian Heritage* (Bangalore).
Shree Purohit Swami (1938), *Aphorisms of Yoga by Bhagawan Shree Patanjali* (London).

STEPHEN, R. (1919), *Patanjali for Western Readers* (London).
SWĀMĪ PRABHAVĀNANDA & ISHERWOOD, C. (1953), *How to know God* (London).
SWĀMĪ VIVEKĀNANDA (1930), *Rājayoga* (Almora).
TAIMNI, I. K. (1961), *The Science of Yoga* (Adyar).
TATYA, T. (1897[2]), *The Yoga Philosophy* (Bombay).
WEILER, R. W. (n.d.), *Patañjali's Yogasūtras* (Columbia) (cyclostyled article).
WOOD, E. (1948), *Practical Yoga: Ancient and Modern* (New York).
WOODS, J. H. (1914), *The Yoga-System of Patañjali* (Cambridge), Harvard Oriental Series XVIII.

II. Publications Cited

CATALINA, F. V. (1968), *A Study of the Self Concept of Sāṅkhya Yoga Philosophy* (Delhi).
COULSON, M. (1976), *Sanskrit: An Introduction to the Classical Language* (London), Teach Yourself Books.
ELIADE, M. (1969[2]), *Yoga: Immortality and Freedom* (New York).
—(1969), *Patañjali and Yoga* (New York).
FEUERSTEIN, G. (1974[a]), *The Essence of Yoga* (London).
—(1974[b]), *Introduction to the Bhagavad-Gītā* (London).
—(1975), *Textbook of Yoga* (London).
—(1979), *Yoga-Sūtra: An Exercise in the Methodology of Textual Analysis* (New Delhi).
JHA, G. (1894), *The Yoga-Sāra-Saṃgraha of Vijñānabhikṣu* (Bombay).
JOSHI, K. S. (1965), 'On the Meaning of Yoga', *Philosophy East and West*, XV. 1, 53–64.
KOELMAN, G. M. (1970), *Pātañjala Yoga* (Poona).
MISHRA, R. S. (1972), *The Textbook of Yoga Psychology* (London).
MÜLLER, M. (1916[4]), *The Six Systems of Indian Philosophy* (London).
NICHOLSON, R. A. (1975[3]), *The Mystics of Islam* (London).
NICOLÁS, A. T. de (1976), *Avatāra: The Humanization of Philosophy through the Bhagavad Gītā* (New York).
PENSA, C. (1973), 'The Powers (siddhis) in Yoga', *Yoga Quarterly Review*, 5, 9–49.
SACHAROW, B. (1957), *Yoga aus dem Urquell* (Stuttgart).
SWAMI NIKHILANANDA (1951), 'Concentration and Meditation as methods in Indian Philosophy', in: MOORE, C. A. (ed.), *Essays in East–West Philosophy* (Honolulu), pp. 89–102.
SWAMI SATPRAKĀSHĀNANDA (1965), *Methods of Knowledge* (London).
THEOBALD, D. W. (1969), *An Introduction to the Philosophy of Science* (London).
WILBER, K. (1977), *The Spectrum of Consciousness* (Wheaton, Ill.).

GUIDE TO THE PRONUNCIATION OF SANSKRIT

(A) *Vowels*

a, ā, i, ī, u, ū, ṛ, ṝ, ḷ; e, ai, o, au;

(B) *Consonants*

gutturals:	*k, kh, g, gh, ṅ;*
palatals:	*c, ch, j, jh, ñ;*
cerebrals:	*ṭ, ṭh, ḍ, ḍh, ṇ;*
dentals:	*t, th, d, dh, n;*
labials:	*p, ph, b, bh, m;*
semivowels:	*y, r, l, v;*
spirants:	*ś, ṣ, s, h;*
visarga:	*ḥ;*
anusvāra:	*ṃ.*

The vowels *a, i, u, ṛ* and *ḷ* are short and sound like *a* in 'cat', *i* in 'bit' and *u* in 'hook'; *ṛ* and *ḷ* sound like *ri* and *li* respectively. The vowel *ā, ī, ū* and the rare *ṝ* as well as *e, ai, o* and *au* are long; *e* sounds like *e* as in 'tend', *ai* as *i* in 'time'; *o* as in 'god' and *au* as *ou* in 'house'. Aspirated consonants are to be pronounced with a distinctly discernible aspiration; thus *kh* as in 'ink-horn', *th* as in 'pot-house' etc. The letter *ṅ* sounds like *ng* in 'anger'. The palatal *c* sounds like *ch* in 'church' and *j* like *j* in 'join'. Cerebrals are pronounced with the tongue turned back against the roof of the mouth. The semivowel *y* corresponds to *y* as in 'yes', and *v* sounds like *w* in 'water'. The letters *ś* and *ṣ* are very similar in sound and can be pronounced like *sh* in 'shore'; *s* sounds like *s* in 'self'. The so-called *visarga* is pronounced with a distinct echo of the preceding vowel; thus *yogaḥ* sounds like *yogaḥ*^{a} and *vṛttiḥ* like *vṛttiḥ*^{i}. The *anusvāra* sounds like certain nasalised vowels in French (e.g. as in 'ton').

INDEX

ABOUT THE AUTHOR

Georg Feuerstein, Ph.D., was born in Germany shortly after World War II and conducted his postgraduate research in Indian philosophy at the University of Durham in England. He is one of the leading voices of the East/West dialogue and since the late 1960s has made many significant contributions to our understanding of India's spiritual heritage, notably Hindu Yoga.

He has authored more than 40 books, including *The Shambhala Encyclopedia of Yoga, The Yoga Tradition, The Deeper Dimension of Yoga, Lucid Waking, Wholeness or Transcendence?*, and *Tantra: Path of Ecstasy.* His most recent works include *Yoga Morality* and *Green Yoga* (coauthored with his wife, Brenda). His forthcoming works include a new translation and commentary on the Bhagavad-Gītā.

Although he no longer teaches in public, he offers several distance-learning courses on Yoga philosophy and history of Yoga through the Traditional Yoga Studies organization (www.traditionalyogastudies.com).

For many years he has been a practitioner of Vajrayana Buddhist Yoga, and since 2004 has lived in semiretirement in Canada.

BOOKS OF RELATED INTEREST

Thai Yoga Therapy for Your Body Type
An Ayurvedic Tradition
by Kam Thye Chow and Emily Moody
Foreword by David Frawley

Advanced Thai Yoga Massage
Postures and Energy Pathways for Healing
by Kam Thye Chow

Trigger Point Therapy for Myofascial Pain
The Practice of Informed Touch
by Donna Finando, L.Ac., L.M.T.,
and Steven Finando, Ph.D., L.Ac.

Trigger Point Self-Care Manual
For Pain-Free Movement
by Donna Finando, L.Ac., L.M.T.

The Reflexology Manual
An Easy-to-Use Illustrated Guide
to the Healing Zones of the Hands and Feet
by Pauline Wills

Acupressure Taping
The Practice of Acutaping for Chronic Pain and Injuries
by Hans-Ulrich Hecker, M.D., and Kay Liebchen, M.D.

The Encyclopedia of Healing Points
The Home Guide to Acupoint Treatment
by Roger Dalet, M.D.

Crystal and Stone Massage
Energy Healing for the Vital and Subtle Bodies
by Michael Gienger